The Coolest People in Art: 250 Anecdotes

David Bruce

Published by David Bruce, 2022.

THE COOLEST PEOPLE IN ART: 250 ANECDOTES

First edition. August 30, 2022.

ISBN: 979-8215812143

Written by David Bruce.

Table of Contents

Dedication

Dedicated to My Sister Brenda

Brenda wrote, "During COVID and when visitors were restricted from visiting their loved one in the assisted-living facility I worked at, a patient mentioned to me how much she liked spaghetti during a late-night conversation we had. She was a night owl like me. Her name was Dee. I called her "Gerdy." Then she would say, "Dirty Gerdy," and we'd laugh. Anyway, on my way to work I bought two spaghetti meals from Olive Garden. I left for work early that night. I went to work, set up outlet dinners in the dining room, went to her room and wheeled her down to the dining room where we had dinner together. At that time, the residents weren't leaving their room and had their meals alone in their room. It was nighttime and everyone was already in bed, so I didn't see a problem. She was so grateful and had enough food for three more meals. It was such a simple gesture, but during that time it meant so much to her and for me."

Brenda once bought a newspaper at a gas station on Thanksgiving and tipped the female employee $5, and the employee cried.

Brenda wrote, "I do remember that. I also remember when George tipped a TeeJays waitress $100, and she cried. Our family does a lot of good deeds all the time: I unload people's grocery carts when the people are in those electric scooters. If they are alone with a few groceries, I'll leave cash for the cashier to pay for the groceries. I've had a lot of good deeds done to me when I didn't have a lot of money. It feels good to pay it forward."

She added, "I just have one more thing to add and then I'm done. I've had a lot of people in my life do good deeds for me when I was at a low point on my life. I was at a low point for a very long time. David, you know what you've done for me, and I can never thank you enough. Martha paid for antibiotics for me when I had strep throat and didn't have money. Rosa bought me groceries. Carla has done so much, and she had us over for Easter just after Chad died. When I say US, I mean all of my kids. She was so sick and ended up at the Emergency Room that same night. Frank gave me a car. And George buys my gas for me whenever he's in Florida. And Mom and Dad were good people. I had a lot of good influences in my life that made me be a good person. At least I hope I'm a good person. I try to be someone Mom and Dad would be proud of."

In a booklet she wrote about Hospice, Brenda wrote, "I used to send flowers to the funeral home, but years ago during the loss of my stepson, someone showed up to our door with a laundry basket of essential items: paper plates, plastic cups, trash bags, beverages, dish liquid, washing powder, napkins, and paper towels. Items I never knew we even needed until we needed them. Paper products are essential during this time. So, I have adopted this idea and now use it whenever we suffer the loss of a friend. I fill a laundry basket full of these essential items. We may also give restaurant gift cards to cover a dinner for an evening."

Brenda also wrote, "I was a Hospice nurse for a patient in a facility, and I asked the nurse on duty to medicate my patient. She said she didn't need it as she was sleeping, and the medications were PRN (as needed). I explained that she needed the medications. She said she can't justify giving her medications. I said it's called symptoms management. She said the patient will need to ask for the medication herself. I tried to educate the nurse, but she was offended and left the room. It's important to be polite but firm. I make no apologies when I am advocating for someone who needs me. I had to call the Hospice doctor, who in turn called the facility nurse who quickly and efficiently medicated the patient as requested. Let's face it, we're not here to make friends. If it takes rudeness to do what's right, I'll be rude."

***

The doing of good deeds is important. As a free person, you can choose to live your life as a good person or as a bad person. To be a good person, do good deeds. To be a bad person, do bad deeds. If you do good deeds, you will become good. If you do bad deeds, you will become bad. To become the person you want to be, act as if you already are that kind of person. Each of us chooses what kind of person we will become. To become a good person, do the things a good person does. To become a bad person, do the things a bad person does. The opportunity to take action to become the kind of person you want to be is yours.

Front Cover Painting for *The Coolest People in Art: 250 Anecdotes*:

https://pixabay.com/photos/woman-fashion-sunglasses-blonde-8729895/

"The purpose of art is washing the dust of daily life off our souls." — Pablo Picasso

This is a short, quick, and easy read.

Anecdotes are usually short humorous stories. Sometimes they are thought-provoking or informative, not amusing.

Educate Yourself
Read Like A Wolf Eats
Be Excellent to Each Other
Books Then, Books Now, Books Forever

***

Do you know a language other than English? If you do, I give you permission to translate this book, copyright your translation, publish or self-publish it, and keep all the royalties for yourself. (Do give me credit, of course, for the original book.)

Chapter 1: From Activism to Clothing

Activism

• During the Holocaust, many works of art were looted from Jewish art dealers, and some of those works of art have recently been returned to their true owners. However, not every case of unethical transfer of possession of works of art is as clear-cut as looting. For example, in 1935 the Nazis ordered Dusseldorf art gallerist Max Stern to get rid of his business. He fought the order for two years, but eventually he sold his works of art at cheap — very cheap — prices in order to get money to get himself and his mother out of Nazi Germany. Given that he was forced to sell his works of art against his will and at cheap — very cheap — prices, should a fair price for these works of art be given to his descendants as restitution? A 2007 exhibition at the Ben Uri Gallery in London made a forceful comment on this question. The Ben Uri Gallery gave an exhibition of the works of art the Nazis forced Mr. Stern to sell; the exhibition is titled Auktion 392, which was the title given to the forced sale. Well, the works of art were sort of exhibited. Instead of the original works of art, which are missing, the gallery exhibited black-and-white illustrations of the works of art from the original auction catalog.[1]

• British graffiti artist Banksy is quite the social satirist. When Paris Hilton came out with her debut CD of music, Banksy created his own version of the cover of her album. Banksy's version featured a topless photo of Paris and the slogans "What Am I For?" and "Why Am I Famous?" He made 500 copies of the satiric work of art, and then he sneaked them into United Kingdom record stores and left them. Other targets of his satire are less deserving. One of his works of art is a large portrait of an elderly and very wrinkled Mother Teresa along with the words, "I learnt a valuable lesson from this woman. Moisturise everyday." Perhaps Banksy's fans are also social satirists. While in Los Angeles to set up an art exhibit, Banksy ordered and ate a pizza, and then he threw the pizza box in a Dumpster. The empty pizza box ended up on eBay, earning the seller $102. What are the goals of such a social satirist as Banksy? Banksy says, "I originally set out to try and save the world, but now I'm not sure I like it enough."[2]

• Activism can be an art form. The Radical Cheerleaders are a group — or groups — of activists who have as their goals "to eliminate patriarchy, capitalism, inequality and poverty and to live happily ever after." As their name implies, they perform cheers in support of their agenda. For example: "Throw those arms up in the air / Let me see that armpit hair / We don't shave or use that Nair / Sleek and chic, we do not care."[3]

• Francisco Goya etched a series of works of art titled *Disasters of War*, which depicted atrocities committed during warfare. One of the series shows a Spaniard tied by his neck to a tree as some French soldiers torture him. Goya's caption reads simply, "Why?" One of his servants once asked him, "Why do you paint these barbarities that men commit?" Goya replied, "To tell men forever that they should not be barbarians."[4]

• Can part of a dilapidated house be a work of art? Yes. In North Kensington, London, author Germaine Greer once bought a dilapidated house in part because one of its walls had a graffito that she calls "magnificent." In foot-high block letters, the graffito read, "Boredom is counter-revolutionary." In addition to its being magnificent, Ms. Greer says that the graffito also states "an undeniable truth."[5]

Advertising

• Dana Gioia, chairman of the National Endowment for the Arts, delivered the Commencement address at Stanford University on 17 June 2007. He deplored the coarsening of culture in the United States, pointing out that so much of what is valued there is celebrity rather than culture. He pointed out that much of what Americans see on TV talk shows consists basically of people flogging products, whether CDs, live performances, movies, or books. Creating a memorable image, he said, "I have a recurring nightmare. I am in Rome visiting the Sistine Chapel. I look up at Michelangelo's incomparable fresco of the 'Creation of Man.' I see God stretching out his arm to touch the reclining Adam's finger. And then I notice in the other hand Adam is holding a Diet Pepsi."[6]

• Celebrity photographer Richard Young once shot an advertisement for Olympus Cameras. The advertisement was supposed to show that the cameras were waterproof and could survive being doused with water, so in the ad Ivana Trump threw a glass of champagne over Mr. Young. His shot caught the champagne in flight. By the time he was done shooting, he was soaked in champagne, but the ad was a great success. A couple of weeks later, he saw Ivana Trump backstage at the Royal Festival Hall. She was drinking champagne, and with great glee, she threw it on him. Ever the professional, Mr. Young had his camera with him and he managed to get a great shot.[7]

• As a legitimate author of children's books, Hugh Troy was annoyed by "as told to" books and other books that are written by ghostwriters. To satirize the use of ghostwriters, Mr. Troy published an advertisement for ghost painters, pretending to be an artist who was willing to paint an art work, then allow someone with money to sign it and claim the credit for it: "We Paint It—You Sign It." The idea, however, backfired. He was besieged by people who wanted to hire him as a ghost painter, and soon copycat ghost painters started advertising for real.[8]

• Portrait painters of society women — and men — sometimes find a good way to advertise their work. In France in the 18th century, Louise Élisabeth Vigée-Le Brun painted many, many flattering self-portraits. People in society looked at the portraits, saw how the artist had flattered herself, and realized that she would also similarly flatter them if they commissioned a portrait. Many people did exactly that.[9]

Advice

• Musician Laurie Anderson and comedian Andy Kaufman seem like an unlikely team, but they used to do put-ons together. They would go to a place that had a Test-Your-Strength machine. Mr. Kaufman would try but fail to win a stuffed rabbit for Ms. Anderson. Then Mr. Kaufman would angrily denounce the machine, yelling that it was rigged, and Ms. Anderson would angrily demand the stuffed rabbit that Mr. Kaufman would have won for her if the machine had not been rigged. By the way, Ms. Anderson has some advice for people who would like to be creative: "My approach as an artist has been to always remember that I'm free. That's what I tell young artists. You hear them say, 'I can't be an artist! Michelangelo was an artist! What would people say?' Well, most people don't care about what you do. So knock yourself out. You're free."[10]

• Artist Andy Warhol was often monosyllabic, saying things such as "wow," "gee," and "great," although on occasion he could speak fluently. When Tony Shafrazi, who became the owner of art galleries in New York, visited the Factory, Andy spoke to him: "Oh, wow! I love the way you look — it's so great! Where are you staying? ... Oh, great! Wow! Then where do you go? ... Oh, how great! I love LA! What are you going to do there?" Tony replied, "Visit my mom who lives in Hollywood," and Andy said, "Oh, gee! How great! Can I come, too?" By the way, young people often would ask Andy whether they should do this one thing or that other thing. Andy's usual reply was, "Do everything."[11]

• Children's book author and illustrator Graeme Base, who created *Animalia* and *The Eleventh Hour: A Curious Mystery*, is sometimes asked what advice he would give a young person who wants to create their own books. Mr. Base's advice is simple: "Sell the TV."[12]

Animals

• Artist Jeffrey Vallance grew up with a father who hated the snails in the family's garden — he would stomp on them. Therefore, on 4 July

1976, Jeffrey gathered as many of the snails he could find and painted an American flag on their shells. He thought that would stop his father from stomping on the snails, but actually the flags made the snails more visible to his father. Therefore, Jeffrey asked his father to stop stomping on the snails, and his father complied. A local newspaper did a couple of local-color articles about the snails, but his father eventually poisoned the snails and killed them. Jeffrey gathered the snails' shells and then mounted them along with copies of the newspaper articles. He then began selling the snails for $200 each and told his father that "every time he was putting his foot down [and crushing a snail], that was like $200 gone!" Money was something his father understood.[13]

• As a kid, children's book illustrator/author Diana Cain Bluthenthal did not have any real pets: Her parents did not want the fuss of taking care of real pets. Therefore, Diana's "pets" were mainly two houseplants. In addition, she carried pussy willow branches in her pockets, and they became her pets. She says, "When their fur fell off, I was so upset. I was truly a child in need of something to love and something to love me." As an adult with a family, she has many pets: a small snake, two pet rats, a tank of fish, and two dogs. During warm weather, the family has many more pets in what she calls her family's "summer catch-and-release program": ants (in an ant farm), caterpillars, crickets, frogs, lizards, salamanders, toads, and turtles. She says, "I've never been accused of having a farm, but once my husband did say to me the place was becoming a zoo."[14]

• In 1969 and 1970, punk singer Patti Smith and photographer Robert Mapplethorpe lived together in the Chelsea Hotel, along with many other artists and eccentrics. She often sat in the lobby, people-watching. One day she sat in the lobby after buying a stuffed black crow from the Museum of the American Indian. Salvador Dali, dressed in a black and scarlet cape, saw her holding the crow. He touched her shoulder and said to her, "You are like a crow, a gothic crow."[15]

• Children's book illustrator Ted Lewin grew up in a household with lots of unusual animals as pets — a lion, a chimpanzee, and many monkeys. (Their neighbors called the Lewins "the circus people.") One afternoon, young Ted made many drawings of Jago the chimpanzee as he lay on the porch. When Jago woke up, apparently he didn't like the drawings — he immediately bit Ted.[16]

Beauty

• Celebrity photography can be an art, and photographers appreciate actresses who truly know what kind of makeup works for them. In 1944, Ingrid Bergman had a sitting with celebrity photographer John Engstead, who had been told by David Selznick's assistant producer William Perreira, "We're going to change Ingrid Bergman's image. We're going to glamorize her ... a new makeup, a new hairstyle, and a new wardrobe, and we'd like you to photograph her." Mr. Engstead set up his lights while Ms. Bergman's image was changed, and eventually the "transforming" man came out of the "transforming" room and told him, "She's changing. She looks great. I changed her eyebrows, added false lashes, and shaded the face." When Ms. Bergman came out, however, she did not look transformed — she looked like the same beautiful Ingrid Bergman. She explained, 'I don't mind trying something new, but I think I know what is best for me and this glamour makeup is not right. I look better with nothing on my face." After the transformation, Ms. Bergman had washed off the makeup and combed her hair in her own way. Of course, she was beautiful and she looked beautiful, and her photographs that day showed her beauty.[17]

• African-American artist Tom Feelings knew that he had to make the point that black is beautiful after traveling to the American South in 1961. He met a seven-year-old black girl whom he thought was beautiful, but the girl told Mr. Feelings, "Nothin' black is beautiful." Mr. Feelings created with his wife, Muriel, such books as *Jambo Means Hello* (1974), which emphasizes black beauty. The book contains this passage: "*Uuzuri* means beauty. Beauty means different things in different parts of Africa. In one, it is a woman with a clean-shaven head; in another it is a great crown of braided hair."[18]

Birth

• On 25 October 1881, Pablo Picasso was born, but the midwife who assisted at his birth thought that he was stillborn. Fortunately, Pablo's uncle, a doctor named Salvador, blew some cigar smoke in the face of the still infant, who suddenly began to move, demonstrating that he was very much alive.[19]

• Artist James Abbott McNeill Whistler was born in Lowell, Massachusetts, although he did not always acknowledge that fact. Once a visitor told him that he was also born in Lowell. Mr. Whistler replied, "I do not choose to be born at Lowell."[20]

Books

• Critic Roger Ebert loves movies, and he loves books. When he is at leisure, he sometimes looks through his copy of *Brewer's Dictionary of Phrase and Fable*, where he discovers things such as the meaning of "Giotto's O," which is this: The Pope wanted to employ very good Italian artists, and so he sent a man to collect samples of their work so that he could look at them. When the man reached Giotto, Giotto simply painted a perfect O and gave it to the man. The Pope looked at the perfect O and commissioned Giotto to paint for him. Among the many other books that Mr. Ebert treasures is a facsimile of Shakespeare's First Folio, which his wife, Chaz, gave him. However, Mr. Ebert says that he will never read it because of its spelling and typography. When he reads Shakespeare, he reads the Riverside Shakespeare that he read in college because it was edited by one of his professors: G. Blakemore Evans. Once, Mr. Ebert tried to read a Folio volume; however, he discovered that he couldn't despite the advantages it possessed: "I tried reading a Folio volume once. Just the right page size, one (not two) columns to the page, elegant typography. I just couldn't. I felt like I was cheating on G. Blakemore."[21]

• How long does it take to write a book? According to children's author Rafe Martin, his book *Will's Mammoth* took either three years or 30 seconds to write. Growing up in New York City, Rafe and his young friends used to climb a boulder called Elephant Rock. When he was on top of the boulder, he imagined that the rock came alive and he was riding on an elephant. For the book, however, he turned the elephant into a woolly mammoth. He worked on the book for three years, making it a long story, but after three years of writing, he had a 30-second inspiration that the book didn't need words; instead, pictures could tell the story in a wordless book. And so *Will's Mammoth* has many pictures that tell the story. By the way, Rafe once took his children to see Elephant Rock, but by then it had been bulldozed away![22]

• Tomie dePaola has written and illustrated a number of children's books featuring Strega Nona, who has magical powers. Seeming inconsistencies appear in the books, which have been created over a number of years, with sometimes years passing in between books. For example, near Strega Nona's house in various books appears a tree: Sometimes it's a bare tree, sometimes it's a cypress, and sometimes it's a stylized design. In addition, a small goat shed may or may not appear near her house. Mr. dePaola is not bothered by such seeming inconsistencies, claiming, "It's part of Strega Nona's magic."[23]

• The books of Edward Gorey are macabre. After his book *The Beastly Baby* was published — a work that author Alexander Theroux calls "one of the most calmly irreverent and horrific pieces I have ever read" — mothers who had purchased the book used to read it, be horrified, rip it into pieces, and mail it to Mr. Gorey. The famed illustrator/author, whose books seldom have a happy ending, was once asked why he hated children. He replied, "I don't know any children."[24]

Caldecott Medal

• Chris Van Allsburg started his professional artistic life as a sculptor, then began illustrating children's books. He has won two Caldecott Medals, including one for *The Polar Express*, and he has illustrated a Caldecott Honor book: *The Garden of Abdul Gasazi*. When he branched out from sculpture to make his first picture book, *The Garden of Abdul Gasazi*, he used pencil because that was what he used to create sketches for his work in sculpture. Mr. Van Allsburg says, "At the time, there were not many books illustrated with pencil drawings (there still aren't). When the book came out, many people complimented me on how creative and original they thought I was for having chosen to illustrate the book with charcoal pencil drawings. The truth was, I couldn't have done it any other way."[25]

• Children's picture book creator Ezra Jack Keats became famous when his book *The Snowy Day* won a Caldecott Medal. He wore celebratory underwear while accepting the prize — his undershirt and underpants were decorated with Caldecott insignia and mottos.[26]

Censorship and Free Speech

• One of the things that Jenny Holzer has wanted to do in her career is to take art to the people, and so she has worked with the written word and has worked to put her words in places where people can see them. One early project was her series of truisms, which have appeared on T-shirts and the JumboTRON at Candlestick Park in San Francisco and the Spectacolor board in Times Square, as well as many other public places. Many of her truisms provoke thought — for example, "SLIPPING INTO MADNESS IS GOOD FOR THE SAKE OF COMPARISON," "FATHERS OFTEN USE TOO MUCH FORCE," and "ABUSE OF POWER COMES AS NO SURPRISE." One truism resulted in censorship. In 1982, Ms. Holzer had an exhibit in the lobby of New York's Marine Midland Bank. One truism was "IT'S NOT GOOD TO OPERATE ON CREDIT." When a bank employee noticed this truism, the exhibit was shut down.[27]

• Lesbian cartoonist Jennifer Camper's postcard "Answers" was once seized by the United States Postal Service, which deemed it in violation of laws banning the use of mails for "obscene, lewd, lascivious, filthy, vile, or indecent things." In the cartoon on the postcard, a man crudely propositions a lesbian. In response to the man's invitation to engage in fornication, the woman says such things as these: "No, but do you have a sister at home?" "Sorry, sweetheart, but your tits are too small." "Naw — my girlfriend would kill me."[28]

• In 1917, Mexican artist José Clemente Orozco visited the United States, taking with him over 100 watercolor paintings and drawings. However, customs officials examined his artwork and declared that much of it was immoral, lewd, and offensive. Of course, Mr. Orozco protested, pointing out the figures in the works of art were not even nude. Nevertheless, the customs officials confiscated over 60 of his watercolors and tore them up.[29]

• José Vasconcelos hired many muralists to create art in buildings in Mexico City. However, some of the murals were controversial, and unfortunately, many Mexicans didn't like them. In fact, a few Mexicans disliked some murals so much that they destroyed them. For a while, the muralists painted while armed with pistols to discourage would-be censors.[30]

• To understand this joke, you have to know that Adolf Hitler was once an artist. The Dutch used to make fun of the Nazis by raising their arm and saying, "Heil Rembrandt." Whenever a Nazi asked what they were doing, they would reply, "You have your painters; we have ours."[31]

Children

• Brian Brooks is the artist who gave the cult character Emily the Strange (who is sullen and thirteen years old) much of her style and personality. Emily the Strange, of course, appears on T-shirts and other merchandise. For example, one T-shirt shows Emily the Strange in a pose much like Uncle Sam's recruiting pose, but Emily's message is "I

WANT YOU to leave me alone." A cult character that Mr. Brooks created by himself is Oopsy Daisy, who attempts to stay out of trouble — but with little success. A best-selling Oopsy T-shirt shows the character and the words, "Oopsy, I said the F-word." Even when he was a kid, Mr. Brooks knew what he wanted to do: create art and have people appreciate it. At age 12, he even had his own company, Brooks Publishing Limited. Unfortunately, it was a fictitious company because it had no business. At the time, the audience for his art consisted of three people: his mother and his two brothers. However, he worked hard at creating art, and by the time he finished high school, his file cabinet held over 2,000 of his drawings, organized in chronological order.[32]

• Children's book illustrator David Shannon started drawing early, but some of his works of art have not survived. He says, "I drew these great panoramic epic battle scenes around castles, but few of those survived because as each person got killed they got scribbled out, so you [w]ould end up with a whole bunch of scribbles." Mr. Shannon is modest. He illustrated Jane Yolen's *The Ballad of the Pirate Queens*, about two women who sailed as part of a pirate crew. Fellow children's art illustrator Dilys Evans says about Mr. Shannon's illustrations for this book, "Painted in acrylic, these pictures show David Shannon's admiration for [famous illustrator] N.C. Wyeth, but at the same time they portray his own unmistakable form and palette." Mr. Shannon's reaction to this praise was to laugh and say, "Well, you can tell it's David Shannon because it's not as good as N.C. Wyeth." Ms. Evans adds, "It's this kind of instant humor and gentle humility that gives this illustrator the ability to tackle so many different kinds of stories with genuine enthusiasm."[33]

• As a kid, children's book illustrator/author Patricia Polacco loved Dr. Seuss' *Horton Hatches the Egg*, which is about an elephant sitting on an egg in a nest on a tiny limb of a tree and hatching it. Young Patricia was impressed that such a large animal as Horton could sit on such a tiny tree limb without breaking it. She says, "Then I started thinking ... if Horton can sit on that skinny, little branch, then any elephant can, and that means I can!" She tried it in her grandfather's small cherry tree — and ended up falling to the ground. By the way, young Patricia had an imaginary elephant as a playmate. The elephant's name was Sweet Pea, and at meals Patricia's family always had a chair at the table for Sweet Pea to sit on. Sweet Pea's favorite book was also *Horton Hatches the Egg*. Today, Patricia says, "As the years have passed, I don't see her as much anymore. I would imagine that she is charming some other youngster with her lumbering and gentle ways. I'll bet they are reading *Horton Hatches the Egg* together!"[34]

• Children's book illustrator Pat Cummings got in trouble when she was a five-year-old girl growing up in Germany, where her military family was stationed. She saw several German-speaking girls get on a bus in her neighborhood. Although she didn't speak German, she also got on the bus, and when the girls got off the bus, so did she. The girls then attended a dancing class, and young Pat went with them and tried to do what they were doing. At the end of the class, the dance instructor pinned a note on her blouse: "Please don't send her back until she's at least eight." Pat got back on the bus, returned home, and discovered her mother frantically looking for her. Of course, Pat was grounded, but she got a good start on her future career by drawing pictures of ballerinas.[35]

• Even when he was in the 2nd grade, children's book author/illustrator Tomie dePaola knew that he wanted to be an artist when he grew up. One day at school, he was excited because Mrs. Bowers was teaching an art class so that the children could learn to draw valentines decorated with daisies, violets, and roses. Following art came arithmetic. Young Tomie was supposed to copy arithmetic problems from the blackboard and solve them, but he used his paper to draw daisies, violets, and roses instead. Poor Tomie got into trouble when his teacher found out what he was doing even though he explained he was going to be an artist when he grew up and not an "arithmeticker."[36]

• African-American artist Palmer Hayden painted stories in his canvases. In *Midnight at the Crossroads* (created about 1940), Mr. Hayden shows an African-American boy holding a violin — which is too big for him — at a crossroads. In one direction are a church and no doubt other buildings and places familiar to the boy. However, the boy is looking down the other road, which curves and hides what is to come. Perhaps the boy in the painting is about to choose a road that leads into both the unknown and a future in which he can achieve aesthetically.[37]

• Maurice Sendak, author and illustrator of such children's classic picture books as *Where the Wild Things Are* and *In the Night Kitchen*, absolutely loved Mickey Mouse cartoons when he was a child, and he says that seeing one would throw him in a frenzy. His sister, Natalie, and brother, Jackie, agree. His sister remembers, "We knew it was coming, and Jackie would grab you by one arm and I would grab you by the other arm, and you would have a seizure." Mr. Sendak says about Mickey, "I adored him, and I still do."[38]

• When she was a little girl, Maud Petersham loved her "Auntie" (her mother's half-sister), with whom she and her three sisters stayed during the summers. At the end of one summer, rather than board the train that would take her home again, she hid until the train left. The result was that she was allowed to stay with Auntie for four years. Later, Maud and her husband, Miska Petersham, created many illustrated books for children, including *The Christ Child* (1931).[39]

• Bob Weber is the creator of the syndicated comic strip *Slylock Fox*, in which the main character solves mysteries by using his knowledge of science. Among the products associated with this comic strip is a set of Slylock Fox Brain Bogglers mystery cards that can be purchased at stores. When Mr. Weber's daughter was a little girl, she memorized all the answers. He said, "When I go out to libraries or stores to promote the set and the strip, she shouts out the answers. I have to 'shhh' her every time!"[40]

• When Margaret Bourke-White was still in high school, her family took a vacation to Canada, where her father wanted to photograph some boys. Unfortunately, when the boys saw the camera, they stood still and ceased to act naturally. Thinking quickly, Margaret threw a coin onto the ground near their feet, the boys dove for the coin, and Margaret's father got his photograph. Later, Margaret became a world-famous photographer.[41]

• Children's book illustrator Lisa Desimini used to do her friends' art homework for them when she was small. One of her friends' mothers liked a sunflower that she had painted so much that she hung the painting up in the living room — of course, the mother thought that her own daughter had created it.[42]

• Even as a child, Spanish artist Salvador Dalí was sensitive to color. Once, his father sent him to buy two tortillas, but young Salvador returned with two rolls instead. His father asked why he had not gotten the tortillas, and Salvador replied, "I got rid of them — I didn't like the yellow."[43]

• A friend of TV's Mister Rogers used to paint trees when he was a little boy. Once, he painted a tree blue, and someone criticized his choice of colors. For years, he stopped painting trees — until a teacher told him that artists can paint things any color they want.[44]

Christmas

• Andy Warhol was an interesting character. He was interested in money, and on 10 February 1966, he took out an ad in the *Village Voice* that stated this: "I'll endorse with my name any of the following: clothing AC-DC, cigarettes small, tapes, sound equipment, ROCK N' ROLL RECORDS, anything, film, and film equipment, Food, Helium, Whips, MONEY!! love and kisses ANDY WARHOL EL 5-9941." His body was in bad shape; for one thing, he was shot twice by Valerie Solanas, the sole member of SCUM: Society for Cutting Up

Men. He also had a hernia, for which he wore an abdominal belt. His friend Brigid Berlin dyed the belts in various pretty colors. When he finally got a gall bladder operation — the aftermath of which killed him — he wore his trademark silver wig during the operation. Throughout his life, he used glue to make the wig stay put. And yet he was normal in many ways. His mother stayed with him until her declining health and senility made it too difficult for him, who spent much time away from their home, to take care of her. He sent her back to family members in Pittsburgh, and she soon died there. His diary contains an entry saying "at Christmas time I really think about my mother and if I did the right thing sending her back to Pittsburgh. I still feel so guilty."[45]

Clothing

• Al Capp, the creator of the comic strip *Li'l Abner*, was born in 1909 and lost his left leg in a trolley car accident when he was nine years old. At this time, replacements for lost legs were made of wood — since then, they have much improved. As an adult, Mr. Capp was able to joke about the loss of his leg. He told people with two legs that he was only half as likely as they to catch athlete's foot. He also pointed out that he saved money buying socks. He used to buy six pairs of socks at one time, nail one sock to his wooden leg, and take turns wearing the other 11 socks on his one remaining foot. And, of course, he was able to make millions of comic strip readers laugh with *Li'l Abner*.[46]

• One of Pierre-Auguste Renoir's masterpieces is the painting *Madam Charpentier and Her Children*. He dined often with the Charpentier family and even called himself the Charpentiers' "artist-in-waiting." Once, he showed up to dine but had forgotten to wear a jacket, which was the conventional clothing of the time. So that Mr. Renoir would not feel embarrassed, Georges Charpentier had the other male guests take off their jackets.[47]

• Artist Edna Hibel simply didn't care about clothing, preferring to wear her old, comfortable dresses. When she did buy a new dress, she let it hang in her closet for a year or two until she was used to it.[48]

• Surrealist Salvador Dali once was invited to a party where everyone was to dress up in costumes representing their dreams — he attended dressed as a decomposing corpse.[49]

Chapter 2: From Collections and Collectors to Education

Collections and Collectors

• Sergei Shchukin collected the paintings of Henri Matisse and other then-controversial artists such as Paul Cézanne, Paul Gauguin, Claude Monet, and Vincent van Gogh when they were not popular. Even Mr. Shchukin had to take some time to get used to their new styles of painting. Mr. Shchukin visited Matisse's studio and liked a still life, but he told Matisse that he would have to take it and live with it for a number of days, "and if I can bear it and remain interested in it, I'll keep it." Other people could not bear the then-new styles of art. A visitor to Mr. Shchukin's house wrote — directly on a canvas by Monet! — some indignant words. Mr. Shchukin commissioned Matisse to create *Dance II* and *Music* for his house. After they had been created, Mr. Shchukin wrote Matisse, "I am beginning to enjoy looking at your panel the *Dance*, and as for *Music*, that will come in time." Mr. Shchukin was a champion of the controversial new art, and he — a stutterer — once showed a Gauguin he had bought to a visitor and said, "A ma-ma-madman painted it, and a ma-ma-madman bought it." However, Mr. Shchukin truly did appreciate this art. About Matisse's *Moroccan Café*, he wrote Matisse that he contemplated this painting — his favorite — not less than one hour each day.[50]

• Wilson Mizner once married a rich society lady; unfortunately, she was tight with her money, and Mr. Mizner was very loose with money — his own and other people's. Their house was filled with Old World art masterpieces, which Mr. Mizner longed to convert into cash, but they were officially the property of New York City — a gift to New York from Mrs. Mizner's former husband. Therefore, knowing that many New Yorkers like a bargain, and knowing that many New

Yorkers think that anything "hot" is a bargain, Mr. Mizner hired some impoverished artists to make copies of the paintings, then he opened an art studio on Fifth Avenue, and spread the word that bargains in Old World masterpieces could be had at the art studio, provided that you didn't mind that the masterpieces were stolen property. Mr. Mizner never actually told anyone that the paintings were the genuine article — he merely hinted in his actions, such as furtively looking out the window at regular intervals, that they were genuine Old World masterpieces.[51]

• In her old age, Mrs. Georges Kars, the widow of a Jewish painter who committed suicide while the Nazis were occupying Paris, owned a valuable — both artistically and financially — art collection. Some people wondered what would happen to her art collection when or before she died, and an art dealer upset her one day by insensitively asking, "Well, Mrs. Kars, now that you will soon have to prepare yourself for the long, long journey, what are the plans for your collection?"[52]

Comics

• In 1976, graphic storyteller Jim Steranko created, wrote, and drew the graphic novel *Chandler: Red Tide*. According to Mr. Steranko, "It's a homage to the great noir films. It's not comic book storytelling; it's cinematic storytelling. I only had a few months, so I lived in my studio. I covered the windows over with cloth, so I could never tell when it was day or night. I ate at the board. I slept at the board. I played only jazz from that period, the 1940s, and that kept my creative blood up." Mr. Steranko also created 29 comic books — this is not a huge number, but in them he used techniques that had never been used before. He says, "A number of experts have gone through those books: one said he found 150 narrative devices that had never been done in comic books before. I remember in one of the stories, there was a man and a woman talking. The woman was suddenly very cold, and her answer was an empty balloon. To give it an extra punch, I had icicles hanging from the balloon. That may seem like a small point, but it had never been done before." The person who wrote the foreword for Mr. Steranko's 2-volume *History of Comic Books* was the great film director Federico Fellini, creator of *8½*. Mr. Steranko sent him a telegram, and Mr. Fellini sent back the foreword. Mr. Steranko says, "Fellini as a kid had translated American comics, particularly *Flash Gordon*, into Italian. In return I sent him the [illustrated book] cover that had 50 characters on it. He sent me this beautiful note back that said, 'I am hanging this above my desk in my office, because I think the magic and mystery of the characters will rub off on all of my projects.'"[53]

• Can violence be entertaining? In real life, no. In comics, very. Diane DiMassa is the creator of the character Hothead Paisan, Homicidal Lesbian Terrorist, who stars in many comics and who gleefully uses violence to solve her problems. In one comic, Hothead and the woman she loves, Daphne, sit happily on a park bench, when a big man sits by Hothead and invades her space by spreading his legs wide open so that one of his legs touches her. Hothead does give the sinner a chance to reform as she looks down at his leg, then says to him, "Uh, pardon me ...." Unfortunately, the big man interrupts her with, "Whatcher problem?" When words won't work, Hothead takes action. She hacks his leg off with a hatchet (for Hothead, coming up with the appropriate weapon is not a problem), hands the severed leg to the big man, and says, "This is my problem! Does this belong to you? Because if it does, I found it way over here in MY space!" (Far from regarding Hothead as promoting violence, I personally believe that the character promotes good etiquette.)[54]

• *Simpsons* creator Matt Groening met one of his heroes in May 1998, after he heard that Charles Schultz, creator of *Peanuts*, was eating lunch in town. Mr. Groening raced across town and went into the restaurant where Mr. Schultz was eating. He then thanked him for creating his very favorite *Peanuts* cartoon, which showed Lucy making lots of tiny snowmen, stomping on them, and then telling Charlie

Brown, "I'm torn between the desire to create and the desire to destroy." Mr. Groening told Mr. Schultz, "Thank you for that strip. In one sentence you summed up my life."[55]

• Some events that might be seen as revolutionary are treated in a very matter-of-fact way. For example, in 1968, Charles Schultz, creator of *Peanuts*, quietly introduced a black child, Franklin, into his comic strip. Franklin attended a non-segregated school, and he went on non-segregated school trips, and this was accepted as a matter of course, without fanfare, as it should be. (And who knows? Maybe Peppermint Patty is a baby lesbian. In any case, Mr. Schultz, his characters, and his readers accepted her remarkable athletic ability, which can be seen as revolutionary — for the time — in a girl.)[56]

• Comic-book artist Jack Kirby once attended a comic-book art festival at a public library in Los Angeles. One of the librarians asked him whether, in his opinion, comic books mirrored reality. Mr. Kirby replied, "No, comics transcend reality." The librarian then stated, "If you were to mirror reality, then perhaps others could begin to understand it." This is something that Mr. Kirby strongly disagreed with. He told the librarian, 'Madam, when you mirror reality, you see it all backward. When you start transcending it, that's when you have a real good shot at figuring out what's going on."[57]

Creativity

• Creative people are often creative in more than one way. For example, Frank Gehry is especially well known for his architecture — he designed the Walt Disney Concert Hall. In addition, he has designed jewelry (for Tiffany's), a vodka bottle, lamps, and furniture. He has even made furniture out of corrugated cardboard. In fact, when he was invited to dinner, he often gave his host a cardboard chair instead of a bottle of wine. When he first thought of a piece of jewelry he might design, he mentioned it to people he was with — they all were rich people. Two of the women said that they would like to have a piece of jewelry like that, and when he told them that it would cost $1 million, one woman said, "I'd love to have one." And the other woman said, "I'd like to have one, too. And I know five other people who would also love it."[58]

• When creating "reverse graffiti," the artist does not add paint to a surface, but instead uses cleaning materials to remove dirt from a surface. Scott Wade has created portraits of Albert Einstein and the Mona Lisa on dirt-covered rear windows of automobiles. In Brazil, Alexandre Orion visited a transport tunnel in San Paolo and used water and a cloth to wash dirt from the walls and create a series of skulls, which he hoped would remind drivers of the impact that their vehicles have on the environment. Paul Curtis, aka Moose, often uses only detergent and a wire brush to create reverse graffiti.[59]

Crime

• Jim Marshall was a great rock and roll photographer, but he could be a little crazy — sometimes from the cocaine he ingested into his body. In March 1983, a woman tripped his apartment's burglar alarm, and Mr. Marshall yelled at the woman and waved a gun in her face. Because of that, he was sentenced to work furlough, where he worked as an assistant to commercial photographer Dennis Gray, who admired his work and who picked him up and dropped him off at his barracks. Mr. Marshall had to follow the rules set by Mr. Gray, who said, "We struck a deal. He couldn't talk to my clients [because Mr. Marshall could be abrasive]. He couldn't show them his work. And once in a while I made him call me 'bwana.'"[60]

• George Catlin sought to paint Native Americans and Native American culture before the West was tamed and their way of life was lost. In this pursuit, he learned much about Native Americans and about the people who encroached on their lands. One night, while in St. Louis, he left the steamboat he had been traveling on and slept in a hotel, leaving on board the steamboat a canoe, several paintings, and some Indian artifacts he had collected. The next morning, he discovered that they had all been stolen. He commented, "This explained the losses I had met with before, losing boxes and parcels I sent back to St. Louis by steamer. What a comment this is upon the glorious advantages of civilization."[61]

• Artist James Abbott McNeill Whistler once told this story about a lawyer: In a trial, a witness was asked how far he had been away from the scene when the deed was committed. The witness unhesitatingly answered, "Sixty-three feet, seven inches." The lawyer examining him asked, "How, sir, how you can possibly pretend to such accuracy?" The witness replied, "I thought some damned fool would be sure to ask me, and so I measured."[62]

• Early in his career, landscape artist Thomas Cole sailed to the West Indies. During the trip, pirates boarded his ship and looked around to see if anything was worth stealing. Nothing was, so the pirates shook hands with the crew and passengers of the waylaid ship, then left.[63]

Critics

• Auguste Rodin, sculptor of *The Thinker*, suffered from rejection during his student days and early in his career. Three times he tried to get accepted into the prestigious Ecole des Beaux-Arts, and three times he was rejected. Following this major disappointment, he submitted a sculpture titled *The Man with the Broken Nose*, aka the bust of Bibi, to the Salon, but the judges rejected it because they thought that it was too realistic. Later, sculptor Jules Desbois visited Mr. Rodin, saw the sculpture, and asked to borrow it. "Take it," Mr. Rodin said. Mr. Desbois took it to the Ecole des Beaux-Arts, where he said, "Come and see what I've found. Look at this splendid antique statue. I've just discovered it in a secondhand dealer's shop." Everyone admired it, and then Mr. Desbois told them, "Well, Rodin, the man who did this, failed three times to get into the Ecole, and this piece, which you all thought was an antique, was rejected by the Salon."[64]

• Not everyone wanted drawings by Pop artist Andy Warhol. He once gave a drawing of a butterfly to Greta Garbo, a former movie star who was famous for wanting to be alone. She crumpled up the drawing and threw it away. He retrieved it and gave it a new name: *Crumpled Butterfly by Greta Garbo*. Another person who crumpled up a drawing that Mr. Warhol gave him was Frank O'Hara, poet and curator at the Museum of Modern Art. The drawing, which Mr. O'Hara had not posed for, was of Mr. O'Hara's penis. Of course, Mr. Warhol's art became popular. In a notebook, he once wrote that he wanted a "GALLERY LIVE PEOPLE" — an exhibit that consisted of people as the works of art. Something like that occurred in 1965 when an exhibition of his art in Philadelphia became so crowded that the staff took the artworks off the walls so that the artworks would not be damaged. All that was left was the people.[65]

• Bela Haas was always welcome in the house of a friend who was a fellow artist, but one day he happened to look at his friend's painting *The Lady with the Cloak*. Recognizing the cloak, he told a friend, "That's the cloak the artist's wife hangs up to keep drafts out." This remark got repeated to his friend, and suddenly Mr. Haas was barred from his friend's house. A young Impressionist told Mr. Haas that it was no wonder that Mr. Haas had been barred from the house — after all, his tongue was so sharp. Mr. Haas replied that it was the fault of the young Impressionist: "Had you painted that picture, first, I would never have guessed that it represented a lady, second, I would have never guessed she was my friend's wife, and third, I would never have seen that she was supposed to be wearing a cloak."[66]

• Artist Francisco Goya detested the Spanish Inquisition, and he mocked it by creating a series of etchings known as the *Caprichos*. One is titled *For Having Been Born Elsewhere*. It depicts a woman who has been condemned to be burned at the stake because she had sinned by being born in another country. Other titles in the series include *Because He Had No Legs*, *For Marrying as She Wished*, and *For Wagging His Tongue in a Different Way*. Yet another etching in the series — *For Discovering the Movement of the Earth* — depicts Galileo, who wrote a book defending the Copernican theory that put the Sun instead of the Earth at the center of the solar system. Goya himself was put on trial by the Spanish Inquisition, but fortunately he was sentenced only to a period of "purification" — not death.[67]

• New York artist Raphael Soyer visited the Sistine Chapel, where he marveled at the paintings — Michelangelo had painted the ceiling when he was in his thirties and many years later had painted *The Last Judgment* on the wall. After Mr. Soyer had seen the Sistine Chapel for the first time, he and some friends saw an exhibition of European and American non-objective paintings. A young woman who was connected with the exhibition asked him (a friend translated the Italian) what he thought of the paintings. Rather than criticize them directly, he merely replied, "Tell her that I saw the Sistine Chapel this morning." The young woman understood. The friend translated her reply: "True, this [exhibition] does not speak to the heart.[68]

• Polyclitus, an ancient Greek sculptor, once created two statues. One statue he kept private; the other he displayed to visitors. Often, a visitor would criticize the statue in some way, saying that the eyes were too far apart or that a thigh was too long. Whenever someone criticized the statue, Polyclitus would "fix" whatever the visitor had criticized. When both statues were completed, he exhibited both statues. The statue he had worked on in private was pronounced a masterpiece; the one that had been "fixed" by taking into account the criticisms of visitors was laughed at. Polyclitus was asked, "How can one statue be so good and the other statue be so bad?" He replied, "Because *I* did this one, and *you* did that one."[69]

• Two Chicago artists, Anders Nilsen and Cheryl Weaver, lived together before her death from cancer. She took wonderful photographs, but she did not want to show her photographs in public. According to Mr. Nilsen, "She didn't want to be there and have to hear people talk about what they thought." Therefore, Mr. Nilsen spent a lot of time unsuccessfully attempting to convince her to show her photographs in public. Actually, it's a good thing he did spend his time doing this. He chuckles and says, "The more I tried, the more she would resist. But then if I didn't try, we'd fight because she didn't think that I thought she was a good artist."[70]

• When he was 11 years old, actor Brian Blessed met Pablo Picasso when his father took him to Sheffield to visit the World Peace Congress. Young Brian told Picasso, "You're not Picasso — you sound more like Carmen Miranda. Prove it — draw me something." Picasso drew his famous peace dove, but young Brian told him, "That's not a dove!" — and then Brian gave it back to him. Picasso said, "It's the first time I have a true critic." In 2008, the then 71-year-old Brian said, "The drawing is now in the Sheffield City Hall and worth £11.5 million."[71]

• A visitor to the home of painter James Abbott McNeill Whistler made comments on several of Whistler's paintings, finding fault with each one. Looking at Whistler's latest painting, the visitor said that it was "not good." Whistler responded, "You shouldn't say it is not good. You should say you do not like it, and then, you know, you are perfectly safe. Now come and have something you do like — have some whiskey."[72]

• Early in his career, Pierre-Auguste Renoir, like other Impressionists, sometimes traded his paintings for things that he needed. Mr. Renoir once agreed to paint a portrait of the wife of a cobbler in exchange for a pair of shoes. He remembered, "Every time I thought the picture was finished and saw myself wearing the shoes, along came the aunt, the daughter, and even the old servant, to criticize."[73]

• When Pablo Picasso invented Cubism, most people did not know how to interpret it. Some Americans once looked at a nude by Picasso in an exhibit and thought it was a fire escape! As editor of a magazine, Guillaume Apollinaire published some Cubist drawings by Picasso. Unfortunately, the public was so outraged by the drawings that Mr. Apollinaire was forced to resign.[74]

• Sister Parish, an American interior decorator and socialite, lived for style and fashion. As an interior decorator, she would go through her bosses' possessions, tossing anything she deemed unworthy — including her bosses' sentimental keepsakes. She once told a far-from-innocent bystander (who was guilty of a gross lack of style), "If you don't do something about your hair, you will be ruined."[75]

• Artist/writer Edward Gorey was a man of wit and intelligence. Edmund Wilson once criticized Mr. Gorey's prose, so Mr. Gorey dedicated his next book to the eminent critic. The book consisted of illustrations only — it had no prose at all.[76]

Dance

• On 12 December 1952, a very young Allegra Kent made her debut with other young dancers on the New York stage. Unfortunately, she didn't know how to use make-up, so in the dressing room she watched what the dancer on her right did with her make-up and imitated her, then she watched what the dancer on her left did with her make-up and imitated her. The unpleasant result was that the two sides of her face were made-up in two different ways, making her look like a Picasso cubist painting.[77]

• Choreographer Bella Lewitzky is her own person. When Rose Eichenbaum was ready to take Ms. Lewitzky's photograph for her book *Masters of Movement: Portraits of America's Great Choreographers*, she asked her if she needed to fix her hair or put on lipstick. Ms. Lewitzky replied, "No, I'm fine as I am." And when Ms. Eichenbaum told her to be herself for the photograph, she replied, "I don't know how to be anyone else."[78]

Death

• Claude Monet worked hard, painting outdoors in very bad weather and sometimes-dangerous locations. Art critic Léon Billot wrote about him in the *Journal de Havre* on 9 October 1868, "It was during winter, after several snowy days ... [and the] desire to see the countryside beneath its white shroud had led us across the fields. It was cold enough to split rocks. We glimpsed a little heater, then an easel, then a gentleman, swathed in three overcoats, with gloved hands, his face half-frozen. It was [Monsieur] Monet, studying an aspect of the snow. We must confess that this pleased us. Art has some courageous soldiers." Monet painted on the Normandy Coast, including the Manneporte arch at Etretat. Some people had been trapped under the arch at high tide and then washed out to sea and drowned. In November 1885 Monet himself almost died there. While he was painting, a large wave struck and slammed him and his canvas and his paints against a cliff and then swept them into the sea. Monet wrote Alice, his wife, "My immediate thought was that I was done for, as the water dragged me down, but in the end I managed to clamber out on all fours."[79]

• Near the end of his life, the heart of Mexican artist José Clemente Orozco grew weaker, and his cardiologist, Dr. Ignacio Chávez, recommended that he stop the strenuous work of painting huge murals and instead concentrate on the less strenuous work of creating easel paintings. However, Mr. Orozco refused to take this advice. Instead, he remarked to his wife, "I'm not going to do as the doctor says and abandon mural painting. I prefer physical death to the moral death that would be the equivalent of giving up mural painting."[80]

• Claude Monet used brilliant colors and flowers in his paintings. When Monet lay dying, a telegram was sent to friend Dr. Georges Clemenceau, who travelled 700 kilometers (approximately 435 miles) to see him. He arrived too late to see him alive; the undertakers were putting Monet's body in the coffin. Seeing that the undertakers were about to put a black cloth over Monet's face, Dr. Clemenceau pushed them aside. He tore from a window a flowered curtain and placed it over Monet's face, crying, "No black for Claude Monet!" Art critic Jean-Paul Crespelle writes, "There could have been no better epitaph."[81]

• A couple of women — tenor Leo Slezak, whose story this is, calls them Fräulein Meier and Fräulein Schulze — hated each other. One day, Fräulein Meier was lunching with wealthy artist Bela Haas, and she asked what would happen to his money when he died. Because Mr. Haas disliked any mention of death, he replied, "I've made my will, and I'm leaving all my money to Fräulein Schulze."[82]

Education

• Spanish artist Salvador Dalí attended Madrid's San Fernando Institute of Fine Arts, where he was a good student. Often, he worked so long and so hard on his art that by the time he showed up at the student dining hall everyone else had eaten and the dining hall had closed. His teachers knew that he was exceptional. To be admitted to the school, he was supposed to turn in a drawing of a certain size to be evaluated. His drawing was the wrong size, but the evaluators knew that his work was exceptional and so they admitted him anyway. Salvador, though young, knew more than his teachers in many ways. He was interested in technique, but his teachers thought that the most important thing in art was emotion. Most of the students agreed with the teachers. One exception to bad teachers was José Carbonero, one of whose students had been Pablo Picasso, but the students did not respect Mr. Carbonero. This shocked Salvador. "The pupils laughed at him," Salvador later wrote. They laughed "at his coat, the black pearl stickpin he wore in his tie, and his white gloves. His skill was unmatched, but no sooner did he turn his back than the little upstarts erased his corrections, which in fact reflected the gifts of a true master. I preferred to keep apart from that bunch of loafers and idiots, and go on with my Cubist experiments." Salvador read art journals and studied contemporary artists whom the teachers knew nothing about. His teachers did not know anything about Cubism! When he had completed his course of study and was supposed to take a final oral exam to get his degree, Salvador showed his contempt for his teachers. The students were supposed to talk intelligently on a topic drawn at random. Salvador was supposed to speak about the Renaissance artist Raphael, whom he had studied in detail, but Salvador did not talk about him. Instead, he told the jury of professors, "Gentlemen, with all due respect it is impossible for me to talk about this in front of these three professors because I know much more about Raphael than all of you put together." Perhaps needless to say, Salvador was not awarded a degree.[83]

• Jay Ryan has learned many lessons as a gifted creator of posters, many of them for bands: 1) In college he learned something wonderful from professor Peter Kursel, who found out that Jay had discovered a stack of paper in a dumpster. Peter advised him to sit down and draw on every sheet of paper. Jay says, "I sat down on a Saturday and worked for something like eight or ten hours, and when I was finished I had this big stack of 300 really terrible drawings. But that forced me to actually make a lot of things and not worry about if they're good or not." 2) From working in his basement, Jay learned to work in an area with lots of headroom. The basement had a 6'2" ceiling, and since Jay is 6'4", he hit his head three times each day. 3) Jay once created a poster for a record. The (incorrect) name "Membraphonics" appeared on the poster; the (correct) name that appeared on the record was "MembraNAphonics." What did Jay learn? He says, "It's a good idea to check the spelling of unfamiliar words with the client before printing." 4) He also learned to keep his posters away from pets: A poster for the band Lullaby for the Working Class is rare because his roommate's dog ate most of them.[84]

• When he was in high school, children's book author and illustrator Frank Asch knew that he wanted to be an artist, but he did not know whether he had enough talent to be an artist. Fortunately, one day he walked into his art classroom and discovered a whole bulletin board filled with his art, above which his art teacher had written, "Frank Asch: One Man Show." That was enough for him to think that he could maybe be an artist someday. Of course, he did become an artist — for kids. When he isn't busy creating books for children or adding to his collection of heart-shaped rocks or visiting schools or home-schooling children or visiting his horses or dog, he answers letters from children. For a while, when he wrote them back, he would ask them to finish this sentence: "The Earth and I ...." Most children wrote back, "The Earth and I are friends," and he used that sentence as the main idea in a book titled, of course, *The Earth and I*.[85]

• Novelist Sarah Waters remembers a teacher who inspired her: Ed Tanguay, who in the 1980s taught art at the Milford Haven grammar school in south-west Wales. One day, he forgot to wear a tie to school, so he had his art students make him one — out of painted cardboard. Ms. Waters says, "He was everything a good teacher should be: stern at times, but good natured; clever, creative, and fun." Not every teacher is good, of course, and some people have never had a good teacher. Artist Dinos Chapman said in a newspaper interview, "I hated every single one of my teachers, and if any one of them are still alive, I hope they read this. They were horrible old fascists, convinced you could beat education into kids, and they threatened to cut my hair because I had lovely locks back then. It obviously traumatized me because now I'm completely bald."[86]

• Architect Frank Gehry learned an important lesson early in his life from Glen Lukens, who taught him ceramics at the University of Southern California. Mr. Lukens wanted to establish a ceramics industry in Haiti, and Mr. Gehry helped him by testing various glazes to see if they would work well when applied to Haitian soil. Once, the glaze came out absolutely beautiful, and Mr. Gehry said, "It's just wonderful what can happen with the kiln and all those glazes." Mr. Lukens responded, "Stop. From now on, when things like that happen, you take credit for it, because you did it. You made the pot. You put the glaze on. You put it in the kiln. You're allowed to claim credit for it, and I want you to do that." Today, Mr. Gehry says, "That was a very important lesson that resonates for me even now."[87]

• After Norman Rockwell's first wife, Mary, died in 1959, friends waited a suitable interval, and then they encouraged Norman to get out into the world. Norman was interested in poetry, so he took a class in poetry that was taught by Molly Punderson. In class, Norman was an original. The class studied some poetry by Robert Frost, who was then still alive, and when Norman was puzzled by some lines in one of Mr. Frost's poems, he thought of an alternative to the class discussing the lines and trying to discover their meaning — someone should telephone Mr. Frost and ask him what the lines meant. Molly must have enjoyed her unusual student: In 1961, Norman and Molly got married.[88]

• When she was very young, children's book illustrator Denise Fleming used to decorate her school papers with drawings in an attempt to get better grades. Actually, her 3rd-grade teacher was so impressed by Denise's drawings that she suggested that Denise take art classes. Denise did take art lessons at the Toledo Museum of Art, and she and her classmates spent lots of time looking at the art in the museum. She was especially impressed by Monet's water lilies and by a landscape by Vincent van Gogh and by Picasso's *Woman with Crow*. She adds, "And then there was this anatomically correct baby Jesus that we all found incredible, especially me because I had no brothers."[89]

• Education is immensely important in art appreciation — it enhances the pleasure of looking at art. For example, at the bottom of Gerald David's *The Rest on the Flight into Egypt*, some carefully chosen plants appear at the feet of the Madonna and Child. They include a clump of violets, which symbolize the humility of the Virgin. They also include ferns, which were regarded as a protection against evil. And they include wild strawberry plants, which have three leaves, making them a Christian symbol of the Trinity: Father, Son, and Holy Ghost.[90]

• The education of an artist can begin very early. Children's book illustrator and author Ruth Heller uses an artistic technique in her professional work that she learned in elementary school. She begins the creation of an illustration by drawing on tracing paper, then she turns the tracing paper over and transfers the drawing to watercolor paper by using a butter knife or a Popsicle stick to rub the lines. Ms. Heller says, "I learned to do that in the 2nd grade, and it still works for me."[91]

• As a young art student at the École des Beaux-Arts in Paris, Louise Bourgeois studied under painter Fernand Légar. In one class, Mr. Légar took a wood shaving and pinned it under a shelf for the students to draw. Ms. Bourgeois says, "I was very interested in the spiral of the shaving, the form it took and its trembling quality." As soon as Mr. Légar saw her drawing, he took her, "You are not a painter. You are a sculptor." He was right. Ms. Bourgeois became a renowned sculptor.[92]

• When architect Frank Lloyd Wright first started offering fellowships at his own studio, called Taliesin, in Spring Green, Wisconsin, students arrived even before doors were hung at the entrances of their rooms. One student, William Wesley Peters, wanted to sleep behind a door, so he went to Mr. Wright's house, found a guest room, took its door, and started carrying it away. However, Mr. Wright's wife, Olgivanna, discovered what he was doing and stopped him.[93]

• When James McNeill Whistler was at West Point, he was a much better artist than he was a horseback rider. Once he was riding in a line with some other cadets, when they all came to a stop. The other cadets stayed in the saddle, but Mr. Whistler pitched forward in front of his horse. His riding instructor, who was well accustomed to Mr. Whistler's failings as a rider, told him, "Mr. Whistler, I am pleased to see you for once at the head of your class."[94]

• Sculptor David Smith attended Ohio University for a while, but he wasn't happy there: "I was required to use a little brush, a little pencil, to work on a little area, which put me in the position of knitting — not exactly my forte." Therefore, Mr. Smith transferred to Notre Dame, but not for long. Before transferring, he had forgotten to check to make sure that Notre Dame actually offered courses in art.[95]

• A sculptor once had a child in kindergarten. For an entire year, the sculptor came into the kindergarten class — at the request of the teacher — once a week and "loved" clay. He didn't teach the children, but simply came in and "loved" clay. Just by watching the sculptor, the children also learned to "love" clay and became very creative with it.[96]

• Landscape artist Joseph Turner (1775-1851) once was walking in the country with the Rev. Trimmer, when he saw a black cow standing against the sun. After looking at it carefully, he remarked that the cow's color was really purple, not black, as it was normally painted.[97]

• Aliki Brandenberg, author/illustrator of such children's books as *Mummies Made in Egypt* and *How a Book is Made*, used to practice drawing her toes. Why? It was too hard to practice drawing her fingers, because she was using them.[98]

Chapter 3: From Fame to Mishaps

Fame

• One problem with writing literature is that it doesn't pay well. Therefore, William Burroughs, author of *Naked Lunch* and *Junkie*, started making paintings when he was old and Beat poet Allen Ginsburg started making money from his photography when he was old. Mr. Burroughs used to make shotgun paintings: He would put paint cans in front of blank canvases and then shoot the paint cans. The resulting splatters of paint created the works of art, which were taken seriously in the art world. Mr. Ginsburg even had a coffee table book of his photographs published. Mr. Ginsburg was no fool: He knew what was going on. He said, "If you're famous, you can get away with anything! William Burroughs spent the last ten years painting, and makes a lot more money out of his painting than he does out of his previous writing. If you establish yourself in one field, it's possible that people then take you seriously in another. Maybe too seriously. I know lots of great photographers who are a lot better than me, who don't have a big, pretty coffee table book like I have. I'm lucky."[99]

• Even early in famed portrait photographer Yousuf Karsh's career, he was well known — in fact, better known than some people thought. Mr. Karsh, a Canadian photographer, took a portrait of Artur Rubinstein, and Mr. Rubinstein was much impressed by the result. Back at the Algonquin Hotel in New York City, he wanted to let two of his colleagues, Leopold Mannis and Leopold Godowski, know about his discovery of a great new photographer. He started by saying, "Way in the backwoods of Canada, in Ottawa, I have discovered a fine young photographer." Mr. Mannis asked, "Could it be Karsh?" Mr. Rubinstein replied, "Hush, please. You are spoiling my story."[100]

• At a time when no work needed to be done, Ub Iwerks and some other animators played poker; however, Walt Disney did not join the game but instead became engrossed in doing something at a desk. At one point, Mr. Iwerks looked over Mr. Disney's shoulder and discovered that he was practicing his signature. After seeing that, Mr. Iwerks realized that here was a man whose ego would drive him to become famous and very successful.[101]

• Charles Schultz' comic strip *Peanuts* was enormously popular and enormously respected. In fact, Mr. Schultz was given a retrospective at the Louvre, the first living cartoonist to be so honored. A humble man, Mr. Schultz said in an interview with *Time* magazine, "I'm no Andrew Wyeth." Not long after, Mr. Wyeth telephoned him and congratulated him on his work.[102]

• After James McNeill Whistler's painting of his mother (*Arrangement in Grey and Black: Portrait of the Painter's Mother*) became famous, he was asked to visit America. He declined the invitation, writing, "One hates to disappoint a continent."[103]

Food

• American artist Wayne Thiebaud frequently paints food and especially desserts; in fact, a critic once wrote that Mr. Thiebaud had to be "the hungriest artist in California." Unfortunately, this subject matter kept his paintings from achieving recognition for a while. In New York, he went from art gallery to art gallery, carrying his paintings and being rejected. Eventually, he made his way to the Allan Stone Gallery, and Mr. Stone told him, "You look like you need to sit down and take it easy. Let's go out for a hamburger. I know a great place." The two men talked, and Mr. Stone asked him to leave his paintings behind for him to look at. Mr. Stone frequently lived with works of art for a while before deciding whether to represent an artist. Eventually, he offered Mr. Thiebaud a one-man show. About Mr. Thiebaud's paintings of desserts, Mr. Stone said, "At first I thought they were kind of silly, but I couldn't get them out of my mind. The stuff is serious stuff. There are layers beneath the layer cakes."[104]

• Mexican artist Diego Rivera loved pre-Columbian art, and he spent much money to collect it. Once, one of his wives, Lupe Marin, got angry at him, so she ground up some of his pre-Columbian statues, then added hot sauce and served it to him for supper, arguing that since he had spent their food money on the works of art, he could eat them.[105]

• The father of choreographer/dancer Bella Lewitzky used to paint. He used food in the settings for his still lifes. Sometimes, a guest would take a piece of food, intending to snack on it, but Bella or her sister would take the food from the guest and put it back in the still-life setting because they valued their father's paintings.[106]

• Louise Nevelson was not much of a cook, although she was a world-class sculptor. She once took her kitchen cooking implements, painted them black, and "planted" them in a garden. Actually, she did find a use for a can opener — she used it as a tool in creating etchings.[107]

Friends

• Sam Norkin is a famous artist whose drawings of actors and plays appear in newspapers and magazines around the country. While growing up, he attended high school with a couple of friends who later became actors. One of his indulgences at work is to put the faces of his friends in one of his drawings whenever possible. Sometimes, this can be difficult. When his friend Salem Ludwig was performing a bit part in *An Enemy of the People*, he appeared in only one scene: a town meeting that featured the entire cast. In order to get Salem into his drawing, Mr. Norton drew the town meeting and included all the members of the cast. (He featured his friend prominently in the foreground.)[108]

• Harold Ross liked author and cartoonist James Thurber and defended him. Once, an artist stalked into Mr. Ross' office and demanded, "Why do you reject my works and publish a fourth-rate artist like Thurber?" Mr. Ross replied, "You mean a third-rate artist."[109]

Gays and Lesbians

• Lesbian cartoonists have an advantage over other lesbians. When Linda Sue Welch, creator of *Out of the Darkness*, comes out to her friends, she gives them a booklet of her cartoons to look at, and she tells them, "Here are some visual aids to help you with this."[110]

• A gay man was stuck in traffic, so he started reading Alison Bechdel's cartoon book *Spawn of Dykes to Watch Out For*. Hearing a horn blowing, he looked up and saw two women in a nearby car pointing to his book and giving him a thumbs-up sign.[111]

Gifts

• Food writer Diane Root met Pablo Picasso once due to her maternal uncle, Robert Albinelli, who fired the great artist's ceramics in the kiln and never cracked a vase or a plate. One day when she was young, her father ordered her, "Get dressed up. We are going to meet a great man." That great man, of course, was Picasso, whom she sat next to and who told her, "I'll show you how you can turn a woman into a goat, and a goat into a woman." He then demonstrated as the patrons of the restaurant silently watched from a distance. However, Ms. Root says, "This demonstration should have come with a caveat, though; every lightning-fast line Picasso drew was punctuated by the purloining of something from my plate. This staccato performance proceeded sans missing a beat: squiggle, snatch; scrawl, grab; jot, pinch; doodle, filch; draw, steal." Picasso then drew and drew on the paper, covering nearly every inch. Picasso knew that the piece of paper was valuable, and he knew that the eyes of the patrons of the restaurant — and the eyes of the waiter — were on him and the drawings. His sense of humor was impish, and after the table had been cleared, and the espresso served, he began to destroy the paper with the drawings in between sips of espresso. (His silent audience was silent no more. They groaned.) Ms. Root says that the process was "sip, slash; sip, slit; sip, scratch; sip, tear; sip, rip. The masterpiece was soon a pile of tiny pieces." However, one piece of the paper remained — the piece that had Goat-Woman on it. When young Diane left the restaurant, she had two gifts from

Picasso in her pink-plastic little-girl purse: some neon bonbons and the drawing of Goat-Woman.[112]

• Peter Paul Rubens was a diplomat as well as an artist. In early 1603, the Duke of Mantua started Mr. Rubens' diplomatic career by sending him to Spain. Because the King of Spain was a powerful figure who could cause trouble for the various regions of Italy, the rulers of these Italian regions found it wise to keep on his good side. The Duke of Mantua sent the King of Spain a gift: a team of three pairs of matched horses and a chariot equipped with springs. In addition, the Duke of Mantua sent a gift to the Duke of Lerma, who was very important in the Spanish court: a number of paintings that were reproductions of masterpieces. The paintings became wet during the journey, but Mr. Rubens used his gifts as an artist to touch them up as needed. Unfortunately, two were so damaged that they had to be thrown away, so Mr. Rubens used his artistic genius to paint as a replacement an original work of art that was much admired by the Spanish court. The Duke of Lerma was very much pleased by the gifts of the paintings, including the reproductions, although he thought that they were originals, not reproductions. Mr. Rubens, being a good diplomat, did not correct the Duke's error.[113]

• Cellist Pablo Casals observed the 200th anniversary of Bach's death by performing at the great Baroque cathedral in the Catalan town of Prades. African-American artist Ashley Bryan attended some rehearsals, and he drew the musicians there and attended the first three concerts — students such as himself were given free tickets for those concerts. In addition to works by Bach, Mr. Casals played the Catalan song of longing *"El cant dels ocells"* at the end of each concert. Impressed by the song and by Mr. Casals' playing of it, Mr. Bryan made a booklet that illustrated the song and sent it to Mr. Casals, who sent Mr. Bryan a thank-you letter that Mr. Bryan describes as "very moving."[114]

• Nancy Miller Elliott was a friend of jazz musician Buck Clayton, who encouraged her to be a photographer. One day, Mr. Clayton gave her a present: a box of cameras and lenses and other photographic materials. He had bought them from a man in the street, and he did NOT ask the man, "Is this merchandise stolen?" Ms. Elliott put the gift to good use. She immediately began taking portraits of jazz musicians. Many of her photographs appear in Chip Deffaw's book titled *Jazz Veterans: A Portrait Gallery*.[115]

• Before World War II, Lucy Carrington Wertheimer ran an art gallery that concentrated on the work of modern artists. Charles Merriott, art critic for the *Times* in London, frequently wrote about her gallery. One day, she offered him the gift of a picture, but he replied that it was his rule never to accept such gifts. Ms. Wertheimer told the story later to the artist Frances Hodgkins, who replied, "Not without reason do they call him Marriott the Incorruptible."[116]

• Marc Chagall and his wife were friends to Sir Rudolf Bing and his wife. Once, Mr. Chagall sketched a vase of flowers, and Sir Rudolf's wife said, "That's pretty." Happy with the compliment, Mr. Chagall gave her the sketch. Later, Sir Rudolf had the sketch framed, and the art dealer asked if he would take $15,000 for the sketch. (He declined, and the sketch instead hung in his and his wife's apartment.)[117]

Good Deeds

• Enrico Caruso did many good deeds. An old friend of his once told him, "I have the most wonderful painting of Naples to show you. I assure you that it was done by a great artist, and I came by it through a stroke of luck. It hangs in my restaurant. You must come see it immediately. You, who are a connoisseur in these matters, will appreciate it." Enrico, accompanied by his wife, Dorothy, and by his friend, did see the painting, which Dorothy recognized as very bad — she even expected her husband to reproach his friend for recommending that he see such a bad painting. Enrico, however, looked at the painting seriously, and then he asked how much it would cost to buy the painting. Hearing the answer — $500, a very large sum of money at the time — he said he would buy it. Later, Dorothy asked why he wanted such a painting. Enrico explained that his friend needed money and would never ask him for it, and that this was his way of giving his friend money. Besides, he would send the painting to another friend as a joke. (When Enrico learned that the friend to whom he had sent the painting had actually hung it on a wall out of respect for him, he was horrified and told him to take it down because he had been "making a funny" — Enrico's term for a joke).[118]

• When the marriage of Emerald, the younger sister of African-American artist Ashley Bryan, ended, she had five children to provide for. Her parents took her and her family in, and Ashley helped her out financially. Some of his salary as an art teacher and his income as an artist went to raise her children until they were grown. The children helped him out by posing for him, although since they were young, occasionally he had trouble getting them to stand still for the pose: "Come back! Come back! Come back to the pose!" In his life, Mr. Bryan has tried to do what the members of his church told him when they gave him a room and art supplies so he could teach art to children: "You have a talent. Share your gifts with others." By the way, children sometimes ask him if he is rich. He replies, "Am I rich? Oh, I am SO rich! I have the blue sky overhead, the green grass underfoot, the clouds, the trees, the flowers!" African-American author Walter Dean Myers learned from Mr. Bryan, "It's about the art."[119]

• Fritz Leopold Hennig, a painter, was a German prisoner of war who was returned to Germany by way of Venice after the end of World War I. As a painter, he wanted desperately to see Venice, especially since he believed he would never again be in Venice. He asked for permission to leave the ship, the *Semiramis*, but found it difficult to get permission to leave, as shore leave for returning prisoners of war was against regulations. However, an Italian officer was sympathetic to him. He told Mr. Hennig to speak only English, then he and Mr. Hennig got ready to leave the ship by the gangway ladder. A guard stopped them, telling them that no civilian could leave the ship, but the Italian officer replied, "That's all right. This is the American Consul who has just been visiting the ship." The guard apologized and saluted Mr. Hennig and then the Italian officer. Mr. Hennig visited Venice for two days before reboarding the ship and returning to Germany.[120]

• Adam Elsheimer, a gifted painter, died in 1611 at age 32, leaving behind an impoverished family. Mr. Elsheimer had suffered from depression, and during the times when he was not able to work, he had run up debts. One of his friends was the artist Peter Paul Rubens, who wrote to Mr. Elsheimer's widow, offering to help sell the paintings that Mr. Elsheimer had left behind. This would help the family financially. Mr. Rubens wrote a friend that "if the paintings should not be sold immediately, we shall in the meantime find a way to advance her a good sum of money ... without prejudice to the sale." Mr. Rubens mourned both the death of a friend and the loss of the "most beautiful things" that his friend could have created but had not created because of his depression and death.[121]

• Children's book author and illustrator Tomie dePaola got a break early in his career when agent Blanche Gregory decided to take on a few new clients and asked him to bring in his portfolio for her to look at. Unfortunately, this break seemed to vanish when Ms. Gregory was elected to the time-consuming position of President of the Agents' Guild and decided that she did not have time to take on any new clients. Fortunately, she did Mr. dePaola the kindness of speaking to artists' agent Florence Alexander and asking her to look at his portfolio. Ms. Alexander did, she liked what she saw, and she became Mr. dePaola's agent.[122]

• While growing up in England during World War II, children's book author and illustrator Michael Foreman remembers how kind and friendly the American soldiers were. Michael and the other boys would run behind the trucks filled with American soldiers in the back and shout, "Got any gum, chum?" Usually, they were rewarded with a shower of packs of chewing gum and packages of cookies.[123]

• Works of art can deteriorate. Norwegian artist Odd Nerdrum heard with dismay that the colors of one of his paintings had faded, so he rehired the model and repainted the work of art, and then he gave the painting to the art collector. Art critic Daniel Grant said, "Nerdrum isn't the only artist who tries to make amends for work that doesn't hold up, although few will go to such lengths."[124]

Husbands and Wives

• Some people don't like their caricatures. Mr. Nicola Ross-Lemeni, a bass-baritone, is one of them. While making his debut as Mephistopheles in *Faust*, Mr. Ross-Lemeni discovered that a caricature of him by Sam Norkin was going to appear on the cover of *The Saturday Review*. He saw the caricature, disliked it, and threatened to sue if the caricature was published. Fortunately, the threat of a lawsuit was dropped after Mr. Ross-Lemeni showed the caricature to his wife, who said, "Why, Nicky, you are never looking so handsome in your whole life!"[125]

• Andrew Wyeth once sold the right of reproduction of one of his paintings to the *Saturday Evening Post* for $1,000. Shortly afterward, the editor-in-chief of the *Saturday Evening Post* telephoned him and said, "We all love your painting and we want to commission you to do ten covers a year for the *Saturday Evening Post*. Andrew's wife, Betsy, told him, "If you accept that, I'm leaving for good. You'll never be a painter." He knew that she was right and turned the offer down.[126]

• Most artists paint professional models, but Claude Monet used his wife, daughters, and friends as models. Why? His second wife, Alice, was jealous. When he announced that he wanted to paint a model, she told him, "The moment a model sets foot in this house, I leave."[127]

Illnesses and Injuries

• In Japan, a popular folk art is paper-folding, aka origami, which originated in China. The crane is a popular origami figure, in part because it chooses its mate for life. A popular folk belief is that if you fold 1,000 cranes, you will receive your greatest wish. In 1943, a Japanese girl named Sadako Sasaki was born. When she was two years old, the United States dropped an atomic bomb at Hiroshima near her home. In 1955, she became ill with the atom bomb disease, aka leukemia. She folded over 1,000 cranes, but died on 25 October 1955. In 1955, a statue of Sadako holding a golden crane was erected at the Peace Park in Hiroshima. Japanese schoolchildren raised money for the statue, on the base of which this inscription appears: "This is our cry. This is our prayer. Peace on Earth." Japan values its artists, including its folk artists. The most revered folk artists in Japan are awarded the title "Living National Treasure" and given financial support each year.[128]

• While attending his junior year of high school, artist Wayne Thiebaud broke his back. While recuperating, he practiced his drawing, and he says, "The more I drew, the more I improved." One thing he practiced was drawing the cartoon character Popeye, and for years afterward, he was able to draw two Popeyes at the same time by using both hands.[129]

Language

• Following the Russian Revolution, Marc Chagall started the Free Academy for artists. Students at the school frequently stated this slogan: "God grant that everyone may *chagalle* like Marc Chagall." The Russian word *chagalle* is translated as "march forward.")[130]

• One of the black characters in Morrie Turner's *Wee Pals* comic strip is Randy, who strongly believes in NAACP — Never Abandon an Adolescent Caucasian Pal.[131]

Letters

• Children write entertaining letters to authors and illustrators. For example, Maurice Sendak has received positive letters ("Dear Mr. Sendak, I love your book. Marry me. Yours truly") and negative letters

("Dear Mr. Sendak, I hate your book. Die soon. Cordially"). He says, "How could you not love those responses?" He also says, "Children are the best living audience in the world because they are so thoroughly honest." Fellow author/illustrator for children Charlotte Zolotow also receives letters from kids. Some are funny, such as this one: "We had to write to an author, and I got you." Others are touching and give honest responses to books such as her *The Hating Book*, about which a little girl wrote to Ms. Zolotow, "How did you know about me and my friend?" Ms. Zolotow says, "Those are the letters that have touched me the most — the ones that say, 'How did you know about me?' — because that means I've really connected my experience with theirs."[132]

• Authors and illustrators of children's books often receive funny letters from children. For example, Gail Gibbons, author/illustrator of such nonfiction books as *Check It Out!: The Book About Libraries*, once received a letter that read, "Dear Gail, I love your books. Right now I am — oh, there's a spider crawling across the page! SQUASH." Right in the middle of the letter was a dead squashed spider. Ms. Gibbons laughed, and she kept the letter — and the dead spider.[133]

• An artist can send original thank-you notes. Cartoonist/author Posey Simmonds once had a Sunday lunch with British journalist Valerie Grove and her family. Ms. Simmonds sent a thank-you note on which she had drawn a cartoon of the Grove family's Dalmatian. It was wearing a striped apron and a chef's hat, and it was stirring a pot on a stove.[134]

• *MAD Magazine* readers are very intelligent. Don Martin's very first cartoon for *MAD* contained instructions on how to tie a hangsman's knot — his answer to the question, What ought I to do? *MAD* readers wrote in to correct his instructions for making a noose.[135]

Media

• Pop artist Andy Warhol sometimes gave odd interviews. Once, an interviewer asked him, "Do you think Pop Art is — ?" Before the interviewer could finish the question, Mr. Warhol answered, "No." When the interviewer tried again to ask the question, Mr. Warhol interrupted again before the question could be finished and gave the same answer, "No." Frequently, nearing the end of an interview, he would ask, "Have I lied enough?" He really did frequently lie during interviews. For example, in various interviews, he said that he had been born in Hawaii, Philadelphia, Cleveland, and Pittsburgh (the correct answer). In addition, people hanging around Mr. Warhol's studio sometimes answered the telephone and discovered that a reporter wanted an interview with the famous artist, so they would pretend to be Mr. Warhol and allow the reporter to interview them. Mr. Warhol had no problem with this. In fact, he once let an actor wear one of his wigs and give lectures out west while pretending to be the famous artist.[136]

• While in New York to receive the Women's National Press Club's Achievement Award for Outstanding Accomplishment in Art, artist Grandma Moses had fun with the reporters. When a reporter asked if she intended to paint any scenes of New York, she replied that it didn't appeal to her. The reporter asked if she meant that New York didn't appeal to her as painting material, and Grandma Moses replied, "As any material." (She did say that she liked the reporters because they were nice boys and girls and the way they came running up to her to get quotations reminded her of the chickens back home running up to her at feeding time.)[137]

• Sculptor Louise Nevelson was once asked about reincarnation. She replied, "I don't believe in reincarnation"; however, she agreed to answer a question about it. The interviewer asked, "What would you like to come back as in your next life?" She replied, "Louise Nevelson."[138]

Mishaps

• Costume designer Edith Head was nominated for 35 Academy Awards and won eight. However, to get her first job in Hollywood fashion — as an assistant — she cheated a little. She was able to draw landscapes well as an artist, but she could not draw the human form well. Therefore, she borrowed a number of sketches of the human form from her fellow art students, signed her name to them, and showed them to the man with the job, which she got. She then began studying how to draw the human form well. Of course, she had a few mishaps early in her career. For example, she was supposed to design the costumes for some elephants in the movie *The Wanderer*. She designed some colorful garlands made of fruits and flowers to decorate the elephants. Unfortunately, the elephants ate their costumes. Therefore, she was forced to use artificial fruits and flowers for their garlands. In 1925, she designed the costumes for the candy ball in Cecil DeMille's movie *The Golden Bed*. She used real candy and chocolate in the costumes. Unfortunately, the movie lights melted the candy and chocolate. Fortunately, a couple of other fashion designers rescued the scene, but Ms. Head resolved never to embarrass herself again, if she could help it.[139]

• If famed architect Frank Lloyd Wright had a weakness, it was his designs for furniture. When he designed the Johnson Wax Administrative Building in Racine, Wisconsin, he also designed three-legged chairs that unfortunately tipped over frequently, spilling the occupant onto the floor. The company president asked him why he had not put four legs on the chairs, and Mr. Wright replied, "You won't tip if you sit back and put your two feet on the ground because then you have five legs holding you up. If five legs won't hold you, then I don't know what will!" Earlier in his career, Mr. Wright designed chairs for another building he had designed: the Larkin Company Administration Building in Buffalo, New York. His chairs were called "suicide chairs" because they tipped over so frequently. Although Mr. Wright thought — correctly — of himself as a genius, even he admitted that his chairs were far from comfortable. He once said, "I have been black and blue in some spot, somewhere, almost all my life from too much intimate contact with my own early furniture."[140]

• Many of Alexander Rodchenko's 3D sculptures are replicas because he and his wife were forced to burn the originals during a very cold winter in 1943 in Moscow. According to Alexander Lavrentiev, his grandson, "They had a small iron furnace in their flat. The temperature outside was -30C. By burning wood, they could raise the temperature inside to just under freezing." Mr. Rodchenko spent most of his life in Russia, and he could speak only Russian. Of course, these facts limited his contact with European artists. In 1925, he visited Paris, where he met Pablo Picasso. Unfortunately, they did not speak each other's language, and so all they could do was to bow their heads to each other.[141]

• Edward Lear, author/illustrator of *A Book of Nonsense*, traveled widely in the 19th century in order to paint landscapes of lands not then frequently visited by Europeans. In Albania, he was sketching a castle when a shepherd visited him. Seeing the sketch, the shepherd immediately began shouting, "SHAITAN!" — a word that means "DEVIL!" The shepherd had never seen anyone create such a work of art before, and he thought that it had to be the work of the devil. The news of the presence of the "devil" spread, and many villagers shut their doors when Mr. Lear approached, and other villagers threw stones at him. Near Jerusalem, Mr. Lear drew some Arabs, not realizing that Islam forbids such images. When the Arabs saw what he had done, they pulled his beard and robbed him of his money, his handkerchiefs, and his hard-boiled eggs.[142]

• When President George W. Bush moved into the White House, he hung his favorite painting in the Oval Office. The painting depicts two horsemen following a cowboy charging up a steep trail. President Bush has said that the painting depicts a Methodist circuit rider charging ahead to spread the word of God. Unfortunately, that is incorrect, but at least the truth is funnier than the untruth. W.H.D. Koerner painted the scene for the *Saturday Evening Post* in 1916 to illustrate a story titled "The Slipper Tongue" about a smooth-talking horse thief. The painting really depicts the horse thief fleeing from a mob of people who want to lynch him.[143]

• Works of art can become lost, and not just in the usual way. For example, a bust of William Shakespeare is thought to have been on exhibit in the outdoors on Lookout Mountain at the Lookout Mountain National Military Park near Chattanooga, TN. Officials searched for the bust, but they were unable to find it. Apparently, it is still there — hidden under vegetation such as poison ivy. Susan Nichols of Save Outdoor Sculpture! says, "I call outdoor sculpture 'orphans of the cultural community.' Outdoor sculpture often suffers from benign neglect, as well as from the environment. We need to become more active and vigilant in caring for them."[144]

• When famed portrait photographer Yousuf Karsh was a young man, he arranged to take the portrait of the great photography pioneer Edward Steichen, but he was so in awe of the great man that the photography session was a failure, and he had to ask Mr. Steichen to reschedule another session. Mr. Streichen was gracious and did so, and at the second session he told Mr. Karsh that he had also been in awe as a young photographer. One hot day he had carried heavy photography equipment to the gateway of Monet's château. Unfortunately, as he said, "I was too in awe of the great artist to ring the bell."[145]

• Early in his adult life, independent filmmaker Jim Jarmusch had a job in Paris delivering paintings from a gallery to other galleries or to the homes of people who had purchased the paintings. Once, he and a co-worker had to deliver approximately 100 pieces of an artwork that was a huge painting with holes torn in it so that the artist could paint on different surfaces. Unfortunately, Mr. Jarmusch and his co-worker accidentally ran over the painting, leaving tire marks on it. Fortunately, the private collector who had bought the painting did not notice anything wrong with it.[146]

• Impressionist painter Edgar Degas was a perfectionist. Once he sold a painting, then took it back so he could improve it. The art collector who had bought the painting never got it back. Unfortunately, in attempting to improve the painting, Mr. Degas ruined it.[147]

• Berenice Abbot gave up sculpture to become a photographer. While traveling from Berlin to Paris, she discovered that she was standing on the wrong train platform. Because she was in a hurry, she went to the right train platform — leaving behind her one of her huge sculptures.[148]

Chapter 4: From Models to Possessions

Models

• While painting in Mexico, artist Edna Hibel needed models, and her mother brought in people off the street for her to paint. This worked well, but soon Ms. Hibel discovered that her models asked each day for money. While painting a woman who sold oranges, Ms. Hibel bought all her oranges, then paid for someone to watch the woman's children while the woman sat for her. Each day, another reason to ask for money came up. Ms. Hibel painted one beggar, then discovered that he was the richest man in the village because he had such a good begging spot. Ms. Hibel says, "I loved the people of Mexico in spite of the games some of them played in order to get money. Most of their needs were real, and they were as generous as they were needy. They have beautiful souls as well as beautiful faces."[149]

• Edgar Degas had some interesting encounters with models, according to picture dealer Ambroise Vollard. He once poked gentle fun at a model, telling her, "You are a rare specimen. You have buttocks shaped like a pear, like the Mona Lisa." The model was pleased by the compliment, and Mr. Vollard writes that "the girl, beaming with pride, would walk about showing off her buttocks." On another occasion, a model looked at a painting that Mr. Degas was doing of her and criticized it: "Is that *my* nose, M. Degas? My nose never looked like *that*." Mr. Degas first threw the model out of the room, and then he threw her clothes after her. She dressed on the landing.[150]

• Comedian Harpo Marx was interested in painting, at one point creating several nudes. He once telephoned a model agency, but he forgot to say that he wanted a nude model. When the model arrived, he asked her to take off her clothes, but she declined. Harpo stripped to his underwear and painted her as she wore his painter's smock.[151]

• Sports artist Leroy Neiman once drew a portrait of Hank Aaron. Mr. Aaron was impressed with the drawing, and he wanted it, so he made a deal with Mr. Neiman. In return for the drawing, he agreed to be a model for one of Mr. Neiman's art classes — the kids got a thrill when they discovered that their model was the king of home runs.[152]

• Not everyone enjoyed being painted by Impressionist artist Edgar Degas. His *In a Cafe (The Absinthe Drinker)* shows a melancholy Ellen Andrée, an actress, and a melancholy Marcellin Desboutin, a painter. After seeing the finished painting, Ms. Andrée told Mr. Desboutin, "We look like a couple of idiots."[153]

• As a young art student, Claude Monet studied at the Académie Suisse, which was located across from a dentist office. Occasionally, a patient seeking dental help opened the wrong door and walked in on a group of art students sketching a nude model.[154]

Money

• A skip-rat is a person who rummages through refuse looking for still usable items. One skip-rat in New York, Elizabeth Gibson, found something better than just usable: a painting worth $1 million. The painting, created in 1970, is *Tres Personajes (Three People)*, by Rufino Tamayo, and she found it by some rubbish bags in November of 2003. Although the painting is large (51 inches by 38 inches), she was struck by it and carried it home only 20 minutes before a garbage truck arrived to carry away the rubbish. The painting had been missing for 20 years. In 1977, it had been purchased at Sotheby's for $55,000, but it turned up stolen after having been placed in storage while the owner was moving. Ms. Gibson kept the painting for several months in her apartment, then she started to investigate it, helped by the signature "Tamayo 0-70" on the painting. Eventually, she discovered a reproduction of the painting in a monograph at a library. Knowing that the painting was most likely very valuable, she built a false wall in her apartment, behind which she kept the painting. She then contacted a Sotheby's art expert, who came to her apartment and saw the painting. The expert, August Uribe, said, "This has been nothing short of a miracle. That such an important painting, missing for a generation, was rescued in this way — and in such pristine condition — continues to astound me." The painting has been returned to its rightful owner, who placed it for sale at Sotheby's, and Ms. Gibson received both a $15,000 reward for returning the painting to its rightful owner as well as a finder's fee from Sotheby's.[155]

• John Varley, a painter who was an acquaintance of William Blake, was generous — too generous. He gave much of his money to the needy, with the result that he sometimes found himself in debtors' prison. He would simply take his painting supplies with him to prison, and then he would paint and sell paintings until he had paid his debts and could get out of prison. He was also an astrologer, and one day he believed that the planet Uranus was having an evil influence on him and he would suffer something bad before noon that day. A little before noon, he said that he was feeling well and that therefore the threat must not be to his person but to his property. Just then, the cry of "Fire!" was heard, and he rushed into the street and saw that his house was on fire. As it burned to the ground, he wrote a paper about the astrological influences of the planet Uranus.[156]

• According to legend, when Rembrandt first sold a painting in The Hague, he received a large sum of money. He took a coach back home to Leiden, but because he was carrying so much money he did not leave the coach when it stopped at an inn. Somehow, the horses pulling the coach ran away when the driver and other passengers were inside the inn. They pulled Rembrandt and the coach all the way to Leiden. Rembrandt was very happy, both because he had sold a painting for a large sum of money and because he had received a free coach ride home. According to another legend, Rembrandt won a bet when he created the etching *Six's Bridge* in 1645. He had bet that he could create the etching before a servant could go to a nearby village and return with a pot of mustard.[157]

• In 2010, graffiti artist Banksy paid a visit to Detroit, where he created works of art (without permission) in four places. His *Kid*

Draws his Garden on Cass Avenue appeared on a wall of a vacant building on Cass Avenue, near the Curl Up and Dye salon, which specializes in punk-chic styles. The hairdressers there loved the Banksy, but they didn't own or manage the building that the Banksy was painted on, and the powers-that-be had the Banksy power-washed off, despite the pleas of the hairdressers. Too bad. Travis R. Wright, author of the article "Banksy bombs Detroit," writes, "That wall with Banksy was worth at least twice as much as the whole property's asking price."[158]

• Garry Trudeau became an adult in the 1960s. He says, "It was the cauldron, the late 60s, when I began to think as an adult. All hell was taking place, the Black Panthers were on trial, students were shot in the Kent State protests, war was waging on the other side of the globe, it was very hard not to be swept up in all of that." He made his comic strip, *Doonesbury*, topical. In order to write about very current events, he kept pushing his deadlines back, thus making many printers, who were paid overtime for their work on his comic strip, happy. Supposedly, one printer made so much money by working overtime because of Trudeau that he bought a yacht and named it *Doonesbury*.[159]

• Louis Caldor, an engineer, discovered Grandma Moses in 1938 when he saw four of her paintings displayed in a drugstore window in Hoosick Falls, New York. He brought her to the attention of art dealer Otto Kallir, who began to display and sell her paintings. Once, after some of the paintings Mr. Caldor had bought were sold for much more money than he had paid, a check for the extra money was sent to Grandma Moses. She returned the check, saying that she had been paid once for the paintings and once was enough.[160]

• In the 1980s, Waldemar Januszczak asked German painter Georg Baselitz, who often painted figures upside down, about the very high — actually, "astronomical" — sums of money that people were paying for his paintings. In particular, he asked Mr. Baselitz if he felt guilty about those sums of money. Mr. Baselitz, who was smoking, blew smoke in Mr. Januszczak's face and replied, "What is better than a painting? Nothing." Mr. Januszczak says, "Conversation over."[161]

• In the 1920s and 1930s, Albert Strunsky was a dream landlord in Greenwich Village for musicians and artists because he was very forgiving when a tenant was late with the rent. Sometimes he would make the tenant move, but it was always into another of Mr. Strunsky's studio apartments. Eventually, Mr. Strunsky was owed so much money that his daughter sent out bills in an attempt to collect. This made Mr. Strunsky angry, and he made his daughter apologize to his tenants.[162]

• Harry Hammond was a photographer of early British rock-and-rollers, including the Beatles. He knew many celebrities throughout his very long career — he started his apprenticeship in fashion, advertising, and press photography in 1934. He says that he was never star-struck by celebrities; instead, he says that he looked at them as "guineas on legs." And for good reason. He says, "I was usually paid five guineas a shot, which saw me living high on the hog."[163]

• Often, we read about works of art being sold for millions of dollars, but of course artists often start by selling their works of art for much less. In 1957, art dealer Irving Blum bought a painting by Ellsworth Kelly, paying $75 for it — by making payments of $5 monthly. In an article about Mr. Kelly titled "Ellsworth Kelly is the king of colour," arts reporter Mark Rappolt wrote, "These days $75 wouldn't even get you his signature."[164]

• Nathan Rothschild knew money, but he did not know art. Many art dealers tried to get him interested in starting an art collection, but he rebuffed their attempts. Finally, one art dealer brought Mr. Rothschild a letter of introduction from an important rabbi. Mr. Rothschild decided that he ought to buy a painting, so he told the art dealer, "Give me a £30 picture. I don't care which one. Goodbye."[165]

• Photographer Andreas Johnsen knows how to find wonderful places to live that don't cost much money. He found out why one place was so inexpensive when his landlord climbed up the fire escape to show him this sign through the window: "Do not leave the apartment. There's a city inspector in the hallway." No one was supposed to be living in the building.[166]

• Early in his career, French artist Honoré Daumier had difficulty paying the rent. He told his landlord, "The time will come when people will visit this miserable hole and say that Daumier, the artist, once painted here." Unmoved, the landlord replied, "If you don't pay your rent now, they'll be able to say it tomorrow."[167]

• The possessions of painter Andrea di Cione were once legally seized to pay off his debts; however, Mr. di Cione got revenge. In a painting of Hell, he placed the faces and figures of the judge and court notary who took his possessions away from him.[168]

• Art will not be suppressed, and a lack of mega-bucks, or even a lack of many bucks, will not stop it. In 1997, Carla Speed McNeil wrote and illustrated a mini-comic titled *Mystery Date!* What was its print run? Only 30 copies.[169]

Mothers and Fathers

• As everyone knows, mothers are important: 1) When William Steig was a young illustrator, he submitted his first cover to *The New Yorker*, and the powers-that-be told him, "We like the idea but not your rendition." They then asked, "Can we buy the idea from you?" Mr. Steig replied, "Let me think it over." He went home and told his mother that *The New Yorker* wanted to buy his idea but not his illustration, and she advised him, "Don't do that! Don't sell them the idea! They'll always expect you to sell 'em the idea." So Mr. Steig went back to *The New Yorker* and said, "My mother told me not to sell you the idea." The powers-that-be replied, "OK, we'll take the cover as it is." Of course, Mr. Steig became an important *New Yorker* illustrator. 2) The mother of Rosemary Wells, an author and illustrator of books for children, used to go through her artwork each Friday when Rosemary was very young and choose the best drawings to thumbtack to the mantle until the following Friday. Ms. Wells says, "My mother would say, 'These are wonderful!' — and just ignore the rest. That is how I learned what was good." 3) Charlotte Zolotow, an author of books for children, used read *Heidi* over and over when she was young and cry while reading the sad parts. One day, she cried so much that her mother asked Charlotte's older sister, "What kind of book is the child reading?" Also, of course, as everyone knows, fathers are important. The father of Tana Hoban, who uses photographs in her books for children, used to keep a glass of nickels by him during meals so that whenever one of his children made a funny, witty, or intelligent remark he could reward the child with a nickel. For example, Tana once used the French phrase *"n'est-ce pas?"* Her sister asked what the phrase meant, and Tana joked, "An old French general." Her father gave her a nickel.[170]

• The mother and stepfather of children's book illustrator and author Margot Zemach worked in the theater. Sometimes, she would look at her stepfather while he was eating a salad at home at the dinner table and wonder to herself whether this was really the same man who had been dancing the role of a soldier or a camel or a demon on stage the previous night. While backstage one day, young Margot was poked and prodded by someone who seemed to be a cackling witch. She worried — until she recognized in the cackling the sound of her mother.[171]

• Maurice Sendak, author/illustrator of *Where the Wild Things Are*, was a sickly child. His father once told him that he might see an angel outside his window, and if he did see an angel, then his illness would be over quickly. However, his father also said that angels were quick and therefore were hard to see: "If you blink, you'll miss it." After his father left the room, young Maurice looked out the window. Then he started shouting, "I saw it! I saw it! I saw the angel!" Mr. Sendak says about his father, "He was as thrilled as I was."[172]

• When writer/performance artist Keith Antar Mason was young, sometimes his father would punish him by grounding him for a while.

His father knew that young Keith liked art and art museums, so before grounding Keith he would take him to the St. Louis Art Museum and say, "Go ahead and browse because you're not going to see it for a long time." Whenever his father took him to the art museum, Keith knew that he was in serious trouble.[173]

• Mordecai Gerstein won the 2004 Caldecott Medal for illustrating the book *The Man Who Walked Between the Towers*. When he was a child, his mother made a scrapbook for him. In it were photographs of famous works of art that she had cut out of magazines. Mr. Gerstein says, "It was my own little art museum, and I lay on the floor and went through it over and over again 'til I'd memorized every picture."[174]

• What kind of a family does an artist come from? From a family of eccentrics and non-conformists? Not necessarily. The mother of renowned American artist Cy Twombly was hardly eccentric and non-conformist. Cy said to her, "You would be happy if I just kept well dressed and [had] good manners." She replied, "What else is there?"[175]

Movies

• In 2008, HBO broadcast the TV miniseries *John Adams*, which starred David Morse as George Washington. Much attention was paid to detail, and craftspeople built much period furniture. In fact, Mr. Morse saw a portrait of George Washington on a set, but when he looked closer at it, he saw that "it was actually a portrait of me as Washington, that they'd made a point of making sure the portraits were of the actors as the characters."[176]

• Film director Josef von Sternberg was an artist. One day, he was preparing to take a full-length shot of Marlene Dietrich. Celebrity photographer John Engstead noticed some dirt on the floor and asked him if he wanted it cleaned up. Mr. Sternberg replied, "If anybody looks at the dirt instead of Ms. Dietrich, none of us are any good."[177]

Names and Titles

• When illustrator Erik Blegvad was growing up, his mother always encouraged him. Mr. Blegvad writes that their home always had lots of art books, and his mother gave his artistic endeavors "only lavish praise and encouragement." In July 1947, following World War II, a more grown-up Mr. Blegvad went to Paris, France, to find work as an illustrator. He took with him a bicycle, many drawings, and 10 pounds of butter that his mother said was "as good as gold" because of food shortages. However, Mr. Blegvad arrived when Paris was full of partiers celebrating Bastille Day, and he partied along with him. When the days-long party with much dancing in the streets was over, his pockets were empty and his butter had melted. Fortunately, he found work quickly. By the way, he and N.M. (Niels Mogens) Bodecker, his friend and fellow Danish illustrator, lived for a while in Westport, Connecticut, where in their studio they kept a large bulletin board on which they put a collection of letters and other documents bearing their names — which had been variously misspelled.[178]

• George Catlin sought to paint Native Americans and Native American culture in the first half of the 1800s before their way of life was lost. One place he wished to see was the Pipestone Quarry, from which the native Americans mined the red mineral from which they made the bowls of their pipes. Eventually, he found it in southwestern Minnesota. He sent some samples to noted mineralogist Charles T. Jackson, who stated that Mr. Catlin had discovered a new mineral. Mr. Jackson named the mineral Catlinite. During his earlier travels throughout the West, Mr. Catlin made a realistic painting of the Sioux Chief One Horn, then showed it to other Native Americans, who had never seen a realistic painting before. Astonished, they gave Mr. Catlin the name "Medicine Painter."[179]

• Japanese painter and printmaker Katsushika Hokusai changed his name more than 30 times — whenever he wanted the meaning of his name to change. "Hokusai" means "Star of the Northern Constellation," while his final name, Gwakio Rojin, which is written on his gravestone, means "Old Man Mad About Drawing." He is most famous for his series of prints titled *Thirty-Six Views of Mount Fuji*. One of the prints is *The Great Wave*, which shows an enormous wave about to crash onto three boats — Mount Fuji can be seen framed by the curve of the wave.[180]

• Very early in her career, American painter Mary Cassatt wanted to get one of her paintings in the prestigious Salon exhibition in Paris. She felt that the judges selecting which paintings would be hung in the exhibition favored foreign artists, so she submitted a painting that was signed only with her first and middle names — "Mary Stevenson" — because she knew that her middle name sounded more foreign in France than "Cassatt." The idea worked. The judges selected her painting to be hung in the exhibition.[181]

• Chicago-born artist Judy Cohen ended up choosing to use a different name: Judy Chicago. She worked in California, and because she had a heavy Chicago accent, lots of her fellow artists called her Judy Chicago. In addition, lots of artists in Los Angeles used underground names in the telephone book listings, so Judy used "Judy Chicago." Her name does have a major advantage. When she returns to Chicago and tells people her name, they exclaim, "What a great name!"[182]

• In 1917, Marc Chagall created his "Self-Portrait with Seven Fingers." It shows him painting a scene set in his Russian hometown. Why is the artist portrayed with seven fingers on his left hand? A Yiddish proverb states that something done with seven fingers is done well.[183]

Nudity

• In 1534, Pope Paul III asked Michelangelo to paint the *Last Judgment* on the altar wall of the Sistine Chapel. Michelangelo worked on the painting for five and a half years, beginning in 1536. Finally, when on October 31, 1541, Pope Paul III saw the completed work of art without parts of it hidden by scaffolding, he was overcome by its artistic and spiritual vision and fell to his knees. The painting was not without controversy. While Michelangelo was working on the painting, papal court official Biaglio da Cesena objected to the nudity of the figures. Michelangelo showed his opinion of Biaglio's views of art by putting him in the painting — Biaglio is shown in hell, with horns, and with his nudity covered by a serpent's coils. Biaglio was not amused, but Pope Paul III was.[184]

• Artists frequently work with nude models. Artists John "Jack" Baldwin (an Ohio University art professor) and his wife, Bunny, once took a vacation in Mexico, where they went to a clothing-optional beach. Bunny pointed out a particularly beautiful naked woman to Jack, who told her, "I am not here to work."[185]

One-Man Shows

• Visual artist David Estey had as a teacher the painter Robert Hamilton at the Rhode Island School of Design. When Mr. Hamilton retired, he kept on painting even though his property in Maine had two buildings that were filled with his paintings. When Mr. Estey asked Mr. Hamilton why he was still painting, he replied that he painted to surprise himself: "If I don't have a surprise each day, I've had a bad day."[186]

• American artist Arthur G. Dove was an early painter of abstractions at a time when this style was not understood. His first one-man show, which was titled *The Ten Commandments*, failed. The show upset some art students so badly that they made dolls of Mr. Dove and stuck pins into them.[187]

Performance Art

• In 1975, body artist Chris Burden announced that he would perform a new work of art at the Museum of Contemporary Art in Chicago. The work of art consisted mainly of his lying down on the floor beneath a large sheet of plate glass near which was a clock. Previously, he had earned his master's degree at the University of California at Irvine by staying for five days in a locker. In the locker with him was a 5-gallon jug of water, and — for obvious reasons —

a 5-gallon jug that started out empty. Students heard about the piece and talked to him through the locker's grillwork. This pleased Mr. Burden, who says, "I was a box with ears and a voice." At the Museum of Contemporary Art in Chicago, Mr. Burden lay still for many hours. The officials of the museum were worried about him and whether the work of art would result in permanent damage to his body — after all, he was not eating or drinking, not even taking a sip of water. Finally, after 45 hours, they placed a pitcher of water by him. Immediately, Mr. Burden got up, went to the bathroom, returned with a hammer, and smashed the clock, officially ending the work of art. He also had a sealed envelope that contained a note that explained that the work of art had three pieces: himself, the piece of glass, and the clock. The note also stated that the work of art would end whenever the museum officials acted on any of the three pieces. By bringing the pitcher of water to him, they had ended the work of art, which, by the way, was titled "Doomed." "I thought perhaps the piece would last several hours," Mr. Burden says. "I thought maybe they'd come up and say, 'Okay, Chris, it's 2 a.m. and everybody's gone home and the guards are on overtime and we have to close up.' That would have ended the piece, and I would have broken the clock, recording the elapsed time. On the first night, when I realized they weren't going to stop the piece, I was pleased and impressed that they had placed the integrity of the piece ahead of the institutional requirements of the museum. On the second night, I thought, 'My God, don't they care anything at all about me? Are they going to leave me here to die?'"[188]

• Being a performance artist is like having a license to be creative and have fun. For example, Ohio University School of Art graduate students Nate Lareau and Marin Abell saw 2,400 ping-pong balls for sale on eBay. They immediately bought them for $80, then set about finding ways to make use of them. One thing they did was to put them in a dryer (on the tumble with no-heat setting) at a coin-operated laundry (with permission). According to Mr. Lareau, "That was a good one. The ping-pong balls in the dryer created quite a racket. They sounded like a hailstorm, and looked a little like a weather system." Another thing they did was to simply pour the ping-pong balls onto a street on a hill. The street was lined with bricks, and the sound the balls created as they bounced down the hill was interesting — like rain hitting a roof. Finally, Mr. Abell and a friend took the balls and a ping-pong-ball shooter and played a game where Mr. Abell tied 10 tennis rackets to his body and tried to hit the ping-pong balls being shot at him. Mr. Abell said he actually got very good at hitting the balls. Mr. Lareau and Mr. Abell still have the ping-pong balls, and the balls may yet appear in future pieces of performance art they create.[189]

• In 1968, on the streets of Munich, Viennese performance artist Valie Export engaged in what she called "Touch Cinema." She cut out holes in a box so that she could wear it around her torso: one hole was for her head, two holes were for her arms, and two holes were cut in front. Inside the box were her bare breasts, which were hidden by the box and by a cloth that covered the opening in the box in front of her breasts. She told passersby, "This box is the cinema hall. My body is the screen. But this cinema hall is not for looking — it is for touching." She would then invite passersby to put their hands through the holes in front and touch her for 13 seconds. Some people took her up on the offer, and one thing that she noticed about the men was that they always looked her in the eyes as they touched her.[190]

Photography

• Leonard Nimoy, famous as Mr. Spock in *Star Trek*, is also a renowned photographer. He spent the first decade of the 21st century creating three books of concept photography as well as working on other projects. In 2005, he published *Shekhina*, a book of portraits of women that explored both their bodies and their soulfulness in his attempt to study "the feminine aspect of God." In 2007, he published *The Full Body Project: Photographs by Leonard Nimoy*, which featured plus-size women. Mr. Nimoy says that the book looks at the "distance between reality and the fantasy of fashion photography where clothes are worn by women who, on average, weigh 25 percent less than average women." In 2008, he photographed strangers in Northhampton, Massachusetts, inviting them "to reveal their secret selves, the self they wish to be or the self they hide from the world. There was a measure of bravery in this by everyone involved. I had no idea what to expect. Some of the people walked in with these amazing stories, stories you couldn't anticipate or make up." One portrait shows a man dressed as a forest spirit. His public self is a painter who creates portraits of war veterans, and his secret self reflects his wishes to avoid "war, strife, and violence of all kind[s], and be part of nature," says Mr. Nimoy. A rabbi wore a leather vest over his bare torso and announced that he was taking this opportunity to reveal to the world that he is gay. A middle-aged psychologist carried a chainsaw that made a powerful contrast to her conservative clothing, explaining that the chainsaw represented her "inner masculine power," a power that most people do not recognize. A heavyset woman revealed her tattoo-covered backside and said that she was "a shy whore."[191]

• When famed Canadian portrait photographer Yousuf Karsh took a photograph of playwright George Bernard Shaw, Mr. Shaw said that he would give him only five minutes to take the shot. Mr. Karsh pleaded for 10 minutes, to which Mr. Shaw replied, "When I said five, I meant 10. When you say 10, you probably mean half an hour. This is likely to end up with you taking all the time you want." Mr. Shaw spoke truly. The photo shoot ended up taking much, much longer than five — or 10 — minutes. During the photo shoot, the two men discussed caricatures — drawings that exaggerate (sometimes cruelly) the features of one's face and body. Mr. Shaw spoke about the best caricature of himself that he had ever seen. At a dinner party, he conversed with his hostess, then admired a caricature of himself hanging on a wall. He felt that the caricature was cruel, but still the best he had ever seen done of himself. However, when he went to take a closer look at the caricature, he discovered that he had been looking at his reflection in a mirror.[192]

• Yousuf Karsh was a master portrait photographer. When Mr. Karsh photographed the artist Joan Miró, Mr. Miró showed up wearing a Savile Row suit and with his hair slicked back. Mr. Karsh asked, "Is this the way you work?" Mr. Miró replied, "Of course not." Mr. Karsh then said, "I want to photograph the artist, not just someone on a Sunday afternoon." The finished portrait shows the artist in work clothes, with spots of paint on his hands. Mr. Karsh photographed Tennessee Williams in 1956, a time when the playwright was creating masterpieces. Later, Mr. Williams underwent treatment for alcoholism, and he asked Mr. Karsh for a copy of that portrait, saying, "I want to look at it and remember, and become that person again." In 1948, Mr. Karsh photographed Albert Einstein, whom he asked, "To whom should we look for the hope of the future of the world?" Mr. Einstein replied, "To ourselves."[193]

• Photographer Jim Marshall had a terrible temper, but he was capable of kindness. The day after Mimi Fariña, the younger sister of Joan Baez, died, Mr. Marshall, grieving, and wearing for once a coat and tie, distributed photographs that he had taken of her to other mourners at her house. In addition, of course, he was a wonderful photographer, both of the famous and the not famous. He once photographed a group of Italian garbage collectors in San Francisco who sang opera as they worked. A famous photograph of Janice Joplin showed her unhappy and tired backstage with a bottle of Southern Comfort. Looking at the photograph, Ms. Joplin told Mr. Marshall, "Honey, some nights, that's how it is." To get a photo of the Allman Brothers laughing, he told them, "I want a laughing shot — or nobody gets any coke."[194]

• When photographer Rose Eichenbaum wished to take a portrait of choreographer Lar Lubovitch, he was uneasy, so she asked him, "Why are you avoiding me?" He explained, "If you really want to know who I am, you have to see my work." He had explained his work to her by saying, "My work is curvaceous because there are no straight lines in the universe. All of space is curved, and so are all of my dances." Therefore, Ms. Eichenbaum decided to take a portrait of the choreographer that would reference his work. She put Mr. Lubovitch in a stairwell, and then she photographed him in such a way that his face was framed with the curliques of a fancy banister. She then showed him the portrait. Mr. Lubovitch looked at the portrait, seemingly without emotion, then looked at Ms. Eichenbaum and said, "Yes!"[195]

• Canadian photographer Yousuf Karsh is famous for his portraits, and he has inflexible ideas involving portraits. For example, he believes that anyone who has recently had a haircut is an unsuitable subject for a portrait. Mr. Karsh was once scheduled to take a portrait of Sir Charles Portal, but he was disappointed when he saw that Sir Charles had recently had a haircut. Fortunately, Sir Charles understood and said, "I always believe that if a thing's worth doing, it's worth doing properly. Let's wait until it grows again." They did wait, and the portrait appears in Mr. Karsh's book titled *Faces of Destiny*.[196]

• Photographer Jim Marshall once took a photograph of bluesmen B.B. King, Albert King, and Bobby "Blue" Bland laughing together backstage. The photograph is black and white, and Mr. Marshall says, "Thank God I had black-and-white film loaded in my camera that night, because the color of the walls, the carpet, and the couch were the most atrocious sh*t color I've seen." He also says, "Why they're all laughing should be left to the imagination."[197]

• Fred W. McDarrah, long-time photographer for New York's *Village Voice*, enjoyed taking photographs of the double-chinned movers and shakers of the predator class at fundraising dinners. He would take a photograph, and if the subject of the photograph angrily waved him away, he would take another photograph. Mr. McDarrah had a satiric streak; in 1960, he even started a small business known as "Rent-a-Beatnik."[198]

Possessions

• Before World War II, Lucy Carrington Wertheimer ran an art gallery that championed the work of modern artists; however, earlier in her life, she knew little about the work of modern artists. In her home, she owned and hung paintings by such artists as Zoffaney, Géricault, and Sickert. Her younger sister, Fanny Wadsworth, who was married to a cousin of modern artist Edward Wadsworth, looked at her collection, then asked, "Lucy, have you never heard of Picasso?"[199]

• When Amy Schwartz illustrates children's books, she will often include favorite belongings. For example, in her book titled *Oma and Bobo*, a painting is hanging on the kitchen wall. The painting is titled "Rainstorm," and she created it when she was in the 5th grade. In real life, the painting hangs in her mother's kitchen.[200]

Chapter 5: From Practical Jokes to Work

Practical Jokes

• Boyd Rice plays such pranks as writing messages on the backs of paintings that he finds in hotel rooms. Often, he will leave instructions for finding buried treasure, mentioning the names of streets found in that city. He says, "I've done this *all over* the world." He and some friends once found a lot of doggie pants in a dumpster. (Pet owners put the pants on dogs in heat so that they don't do anything that will result in the birth of puppies.) He and his friends walked all around the neighborhood, putting doggie pants on every dog they could. One of his friends wanted fruit pie at a restaurant that advertised that it had fruit pie, but every time the friend asked for fruit pie, the servers at the restaurant said that they were out of fruit pie. Therefore, one day Mr. Rice and a number of his friends kept telephoning the restaurant and asking if it had fruit pie. The following day, he and his friends, including the friend who had long wanted fruit pie at the restaurant, went to the restaurant and sure enough, it had stocked many kinds of fruit pie. Mr. Rice's friend was very happy. In addition, Mr. Rice and a few artist friends named Laurie O'Connell, Steve Thomsen, and Jeffrey Vallance once had an art show at the Otis Art Institute on Wilshire Boulevard in Los Angeles. They called themselves the Mezoic Group, from the word "Mesozoic." However, instead of exhibiting their own works of art, they exhibited paintings that they had bought at thrift stores. Actually, Mr. Rice regarded these paintings as real paintings. He says that "it was one of the best art shows I've ever seen. It was real people doing real paintings, and they turned out odder and more distorted than if someone were deliberately *trying* to create really unusual art." As you may expect, some of the people who came to the art show were angry. One person complained, "This is blasphemy! This gallery space should be given to serious people trying to say something worthwhile."[201]

• When Frida Kahlo was a young student, she and some of her friends used to play practical jokes on and torment famous muralist Diego Rivera, whom she later married. Mr. Rivera even started to wear a pistol so that he could frighten his tormenters into behaving. Mr. Rivera was a man of great size and great passion and great impetuosity. At a party, he once decided that he did not like the record that was being played, so he shot the record player.[202]

• Even as a boy, Renaissance painter Giotto di Bondone exhibited remarkable talent. He was apprenticed to the painter Cimabue (the nickname means "ox head"), and once, after Cimabue had painted a figure, Giotto painted a fly on the figure's nose. The fly was so realistic that Cimabue waved his hand at the fly to chase it away.[203]

• When Hugh Troy was a student at Cornell, he once took a pair of galoshes that belonged to a professor and painted them to resemble human feet, then he covered them with lampblack. The next time it rained, the rain washed off the lampblack and the professor appeared to be walking in the rain in his bare feet.[204]

Prejudice

• Georgia O'Keefe ran into prejudice when she created serious art at a time when many Americans did not think that women could create serious art. At the Art Institute of Chicago, seeing live models — nude — shocked her and made her want to stop taking anatomy lessons, and at the Art Students League in New York, a male student told her that she ought to be his live model. After all, he said, he was going to be a serious artist and she would end up teaching art to females. Another student painted over her art because she had not painted trees in the Impressionist style. Actually, Ms. O'Keefe did not care how the Impressionist painted trees — she was too busy creating her own style — a style that would make her a world-famous artist.[205]

• Mexican artists Diego Rivera and Frida Kahlo once stayed at a hotel in Detroit, but they discovered that no Jews were permitted there. Mr. Rivera shouted, "But Frida and I have Jewish blood! We are going to have to leave!" In fact, they did have Jewish blood. His paternal grandfather had married a Mexican of Portuguese-Jewish descent, and Frida's mother was a Jewish Hungarian immigrant. Because Diego and Frida were international celebrities, the hotel immediately changed its policy.[206]

• Early in his life, African-American artist Palmer Hayden wanted some experience working with an established artist, so he placed this ad in a newspaper: "Young artist would like a job as an assistant to commercial artist." A commercial artist did want to interview him, but when Mr. Hayden showed up for the job interview, the commercial artist said, "Oh, I didn't know you were colored." End of interview. Despite such treatment, Mr. Hayden kept on creating art.[207]

• For a long time, Edgar Degas thought that women did not know what style was, but when he saw Mary Cassatt's 1886 painting titled *Girl Arranging Her Hair*, he changed his mind. In fact, he traded one of his own paintings for her painting, and he kept *Girl Arranging Her Hair* until he died.[208]

Problem-Solving

• Pakistani Nigar Nazar uses cartoons to spread a female-positive message. One of her characters is a perky, 20-something female named Gogi, who wears polka-dotted clothing. Among the many places in which her work appears is buses, for which she designs public murals. Ms. Nazar points out that females have opportunities for education and much freedom in Pakistani cities: "Girls are doing very well in Pakistan, I must say. I mean, there are women in just about every field you can imagine. They are diplomats, they are vice chancellors, they are in the police, they are in the air force, they are pilots." Unfortunately, in rural areas those opportunities are lacking. This has led to a problem. Ms. Nazar explains, "We have this staring problem. Especially from the rural areas, when [the men] come from the rural areas into the city, they just find it odd that women should be freely moving around and all that. So they get in the habit of staring, and it's very annoying."

Therefore, to combat the problem, she designed a mural on that topic. However, she understood that some people, including clergy, very conservative men, and mullahs, might object to the mural, so she read the Quran and found a passage that — translated from the Arabic to Urdu (Pakistan's official language) — she put on the mural. In English, this is the passage: "Oh, ye believers, tell these men to lower their gaze, for we know what is in their hearts." She says, "The clergy loved it. The mullahs loved it. … It was the talk of the town."[209]

• Costume designer Edith Head and actress Bette Davis worked together in many films, with good results. Still, mishaps occurred. Fortunately, with some problem-solving the mishaps sometimes resulted in improvements to the costumes. For the film *All About Eve*, Ms. Head designed a dress with a square neckline, but when the dress was finished (the night before the scene was to be shot, due to a tight deadline) and Ms. Davis put it on before filming a scene, the neckline was too big for her. To fix the dress would take time, and that meant that filming the scene had to be delayed. However, Ms. Head told Ms. Davis that she would tell the director, Joe Mankiewicz, what had happened. But Ms. Davis called Ms. Head back before she left the dressing room. Ms. Davis had pulled the neckline of the dress off her shoulders. She asked Ms. Head, "Don't you like it better like this, anyway?" Ms. Head says, "It looked wonderful, and I could have hugged her. In fact, I think I did." Ms. Davis' off-the-shoulder dress is a well-loved movie costume.[210]

• Many artists are impoverished early in their careers. When Pablo Picasso was living with Fernande Olivier, they sometimes ran out of money to buy food. One trick they used to get food was to order it and have it delivered. When the delivery boy would knock on their door with bags of food, Ms. Olivier would yell, "Put them down! I can't open [the door] now! I'm naked!" The delivery boy would put down the bags of food and leave, Mr. Picasso and Ms. Olivier would eat, and when they got the money, they would pay for the food. Even earlier, when Mr. Picasso lived in an unfurnished apartment with his friend Carlos Casagemas, they could not afford to buy or rent furniture, and so Mr. Picasso painted fine furniture on the walls. He even painted a maid and an errand boy. (By the way, young Pablo grew up watching his artist father create art. Reportedly, Pablo's first word was *piz* — the Spanish word for pencil is *lápiz*.)[211]

• While dancing in the Soviet Union, Balanchine ballerina Allegra Kent saw some imperial crowns with finely detailed work that had been created before the invention of magnifying glasses. How could such finely detailed work be done without a magnifying glass? The goldsmiths had used a glass of water. Looking through the water created a magnifying effect that helped the goldsmiths do their finely detailed work. Remembering this lesson, in later years, when Ms. Kent was in a restaurant and had forgotten to bring her eyeglasses, she would hold up a glass of white wine and read the menu through it.[212]

• During his lifetime, the murals of Mexican artist Diego Rivera were controversial and often censored — sometimes even defaced. After he died, however, enormous effort was taken to preserve them for posterity. For example, the Hotel del Prado in Mexico City is the proud owner of one of Mr. Rivera's murals. Unfortunately, because of earthquake tremors the hotel's foundation shifted, cracking the fresco. Therefore, the hotel moved the fresco — all nine tons of it! — to a different location, where it is safe.[213]

• Andy Warhol hated to throw anything away, and he solved the problem of what to do with his stuff by creating "Time Capsules." He kept a box on which he wrote "T.C." and a date, and each day he would drop stuff into the box: junk mail, gallery announcements, letters from famous people, and other odds and ends. When the box was filled, it was sealed with tape and stored. Then he began filling another box. Today many of the Time Capsules are in the Andy Warhol Museum in Pittsburgh, PA.[214]

• Norman Rockwell used children as live models for his paintings, but sometimes they grew fidgety. He found a way to help keep them still. He paid the children 50 cents per hour, with the child model posing for 25 minutes and then taking a 5-minute break. At the start of a modeling session, Mr. Rockwell would put a pile of nickels on a table, and at the end of each 25-minute modeling period, he put five nickels in a stack to show the child how much money the child had earned.[215]

• When famed architect Frank Lloyd Wright designed the Johnson Wax Administrative Building in Racine, Wisconsin, he put unusual columns in the central open work space. Unfortunately, he could not get a permit to build the columns because other people thought that the columns would be unable to support the weight they were supposed to support. Mr. Wright was able to convince these people that the columns were safe by building one column, then demonstrating that it could support three times the weight it was supposed to support.[216]

• Architect Frank Lloyd Wright concerned himself with fire protection throughout his career, in part because his own studio, called Taliesin, in Spring Green, Wisconsin, burned down three times. When the Great Kanto Earthquake struck Tokyo in 1923, fire broke out at the Wright-designed Imperial Hotel. However, the fire was put out quickly with water from the pool near the front entrance — Mr. Wright had placed the pool there specifically in case of fire.[217]

• Al Capp, the cartoonist of *Li'l Abner*, was a master at keeping his audience interested in his comic strip. He always made sure that the storylines of his comic strip ended on Wednesdays. That way, he had a few days to build up audience interest in a new storyline before the Sunday hiatus. Mr. Capp once explained, "If I ended one on a Saturday, millions of my readers would have nothing to worry about over the weekend and would forget me and turn to *Popeye*."[218]

• *Architecture* magazine once hired Margaret Bourke-White to take some photographs of a new schoolhouse that was being constructed. She looked over the scene, but although the schoolhouse was impressive, the rubbish of construction marred its location. No problem. She cleared away what rubbish she could, then visited a florist shop to buy flowers to stick in the muddy ground and make it look attractive.[219]

• The Renaissance painter Raphael (1483-1520) was supposed to paint the first floor of the palace of his friend Agostini Chigi, but Raphael fell in love and because of the time he spent wooing his lady love, his friend despaired of ever having his palace painted. Fortunately, Mr. Chigi solved the problem by having Raphael's lady love move into his palace until the painting was completed.[220]

• Impressionist painter Claude Monet wanted to paint a large canvas measuring eight feet by seven feet. Normally, this would not be a problem, but Monet wanted to paint it outdoors, and he had to figure out a way to reach all parts of the canvas. Eventually, he dug a trench in the ground so that he could raise or lower the painting as needed.[221]

• In 1977, Pop artist Andy Warhol attended a dinner given at the White House by President Gerald Ford. Mr. Warhol wore a formal white jacket and pants, and a white tie. Because the dress pants itched, underneath them Mr. Warhol wore a pair of blue jeans.[222]

Royalty

• When Queen Hatshepsut ruled ancient Egypt, it was the world's most powerful nation. When her father, Thutmose I, died without a male heir, she married her half brother, as was common in Egypt's royal family then, and they ruled Egypt together. Her husband, Thutmose II, died after ten years of marriage, and his son by a concubine became Pharaoh Thutmose III. He was still a child, so Queen Hatshepsut became regent of Egypt. However, after seven years as regent, she named herself the King of Egypt. Because males dominated ancient Egyptian society, and because she wanted to reassure the ancient

Egyptians that the kingship was in good hands, Queen Hatshepsut made sure artists portrayed her as a man. Ancient Egyptian works of art show her wearing the false beard that pharaohs wore, and they show her without breasts. She was also called "His Majesty," although ancient scribes sometimes referred to her as "His Majesty, herself." Most Egyptologists give her high marks because during her twenty-year reign Egypt was both prosperous and peaceful.[223]

• Celebrity photographer Richard Young was in Tangiers, Morocco, to shoot Malcolm Forbes' 70th birthday party. The morning after the party, Mr. Young learned that his flight back to London had been delayed. He saw King Constantine of Greece walking to his private plane, so he called to him, "Good morning, sir. Is there any chance of a lift back to London? I'm delayed." The king waved to him, but kept on walking. The captain of the plane then approached Mr. Young and said, "King Constantine would love to give you a lift to London, but sadly he is flying to Austria."[224]

• Author and artist Edward Lear, of *A Book of Nonsense* fame, once gave a series of art lessons to Queen Victoria. Of course, coming from a family who had been royalty for a very long time, she had many, many portraits and other works of art hanging in the palace. One day, she took Mr. Lear on a tour of the palace, showing him many of the works of art there. He was amazed at such a wealth of art and exclaimed, "Oh! Where did you get all these beautiful things?" Queen Victoria replied, "I inherited them."[225]

Vehicles

• David Byrne, former head of the Talking Heads, is a writer and artist as well as a musician. In 2009, he published *The Bicycle Diaries*, a book about his bicycling in urban areas. As an artist, he has designed bicycle-locking posts for use in New York City. Each is designed for the area in which it will be used. At the Museum of Modern Art, the bicycle-locking post is a blob. At the Ladies' Mile, the bicycle-locking post is a high heel. Mr. Byrne says, "They were doodles I did for the amusement of the Department of Transportation [DOT]. Their response was, 'We love these. If you can produce them, we have the authority to put them up.'"[226]

• Mike Sheehan loved his 1969 Ferrari convertible so much that he wanted to keep it near him forever in his Costa Mesa, California, home. In 1982, he enlisted the help of a professional artist and had the car crushed into a chunk that the artist pounded into shape and painted a bright red, then added a base and a glass top. The result? Mr. Sheehan owned a 2' by 2' by 4', 1000-pound table.[227]

• Cartoonist Will Elder, who has worked for *MAD* magazine, grew up poor. He double-dated with a friend who owned a car. When the date was over, and Will had to be dropped off, the friend would let him out in front of a very nice house, and leave. Will then walked the rest of the way to his own home, which was not a very nice house.[228]

War

• War sometimes has unexpected results. For example, Michael Foreman, the author and illustrator of many books for children, was a child in England during World War II, and he lived in a town that housed POWs. The POWs worked on the farms near the village, and they would participate in games of soccer. Some of the POWs married English women. For example, a German POW married Michael's cousin Gwen. When the Germans bombed the town, many gardens were destroyed along with many buildings, resulting in the scattering of seeds. Growing among heaps of rubble could be found flowers such as marigolds and irises. Also growing among the heaps of rubble was something very valuable during wartime: potatoes. During the blackouts to prevent bombs from being dropped on buildings, a danger arose from accidents because people were driving vehicles without using the lights. Therefore, men were encouraged to leave their shirttails out while walking at night because the light color of the shirt would show up better at night than the men's usually dark jackets. A farmer even painted white stripes on his cows just in case they wandered onto a road. In addition, the cards that came inside packs of cigarettes became a source of valuable information as the cards explained such things as how to wear a gas mask properly and how to dispose of incendiary bombs. By the way, a sailor once let a very young Michael take a puff on a cigarette, and Michael has never smoked since.[229]

• British abstract painter Terry Frost became an artist in World War II. He was taken prisoner of war, and he spent four years as a POW. In Stalag 383 in Germany, Mr. Frost met Adrian Heath, a painter who inspired him. To paint, Mr. Heath and Mr. Frost used brushes made of horse hairs. For paint, they mixed pigment with oil from sardine cans. Boredom was a problem in the POW camps, and the prisoners once started competing in an imaginary Olympics. Mr. Frost's son Anthony says that "the Germans thought they'd gone mad, so they took them for a walk. Dad always said he couldn't stand those walks — the freedom without freedom. But he made sure he took in every flower, every leaf."[230]

• War can be horrible. During World War I, French painter Edouard Manet reported that at the butcher shops people were buying dogs, cats, and rats. In addition, no cabs were running because the horses that pulled them had all been eaten.[231]

Wit

• Banksy, the British graffiti artist, makes fun of real people and of art. In 2003, at a London anti-war demonstration, he passed out signs that stated, "I Don't Believe In Anything. I'm Just Here for the Violence." He has smuggled his works of art into major museums and left them there. For example, he put a version of the *Mona Lisa* (with a smiley face) in the Louvre, and he put a beautiful country landscape (sectioned off by police crime-scene tape) in the Tate. Banksy's art sells quite well. Ralph Taylor, who works in contemporary art for Sotheby's, said about him, "He is the quickest-growing artist anyone has ever seen of all time." After Sotheby's held a sale of his art, Banksy posted a painting on his Web site. The painting showed an auctioneer and a crowd of bidders, and it has this caption: "I can't believe you morons actually buy this sh[*]t."[232]

• Famous British graffiti (and fine) artist Banksy is witty. He once smuggled a piece of rock art (showing a Stone Age hunter — and a shopping cart) into the British Museum — his credit on the art was "Banksyus Maximus." He also once put a parody of Any Warhol's Pop Art Campbell's soup cans into New York's Museum of Modern Art — Banksy's parody showed a can of Tesco Value cream of tomato soup. In addition, Banksy once created an open-air sculpture by putting shark fins in a pond in east London's Victoria Park.[233]

• Al Capp, the cartoonist of *Li'l Abner*, frequently lectured. He especially enjoyed question-and-answer sessions, and before his lectures audience members would be given index cards on which were printed this message: "Al Capp Is An Expert On Nothing But Has An Opinion On Everything. What Is Your Question?" He would compose witty and/or thought-provoking answers to the questions, then deliver them at the public-speaking event. For example: "Are you for or against euthanasia? A: For whom? Clarify."[234]

• Henry Fuseli was a teacher of art, and he was a wit. He once examined a student's work of "art" and said, "It is bad. Take it to the woods and shoot it. That's a good boy." Once, his own painting titled *The Miracle of the Loaves and Fishes* was criticized. Someone said that the boat was too small. Mr. Fuseli replied, "That's part of the miracle."[235]

Work

• Henri Matisse worked long and hard at his art. He said to fellow artist André Verdet in 1952, "If people knew what Matisse, supposedly the painter of happiness, had gone through, the anguish and tragedy he had to overcome to manage to capture that light which has never left him, if people knew all that, they would also realize that this happiness, this light, this dispassionate wisdom which seems to be mine, are sometimes well deserved, given the severity of my trials." Please don't think that Matisse chose to talk about art rather than make art. Painter George L.K. Morris met Matisse by chance on a train and tried to start a conversation about art, but Matisse told him that "all artists should have their tongues cut out — then they'd have more time for work." Matisse even stuck his tongue out at Mr. Morris and made a cutting motion with his fingers. One artist Matisse did talk to was Pablo Picasso, to whom he said, "We must talk to each other as much as we can. When one of us dies, there will be some things the other will never be able to talk of with anyone else." (When Matisse died, Picasso said, "Now I have to work for the both of us.") Matisse need not have been a painter; other careers that he thought he would enjoy included actor, jockey, and violinist. However, when he was a child, he did not want to be a violinist. His father wanted him to take violin lessons, and to share the cost of the teacher he convinced the father of a boy next door to have his son take lessons at the same time as young Matisse. But when the violin teacher arrived at Matisse's house to give the boys a lesson, young Matisse would climb over the fence into the other boy's yard. And when the violin teacher went next door to search for the boys, the boys would climb the fence to get into young Matisse's yard. By the way, at age 44 Matisse decided to study the violin. To avoid annoying his neighbors, he practiced in the bathroom.[236]

• The art of Howard Hodgkin is loved by the public. Early in his life, he knew that he wanted to be an artist, and he ran away from nearly every school he was sent to. Once, a police officer asked him why he had run away from a school: "Why did you do this? Are they maltreating you?" The young Howard replied, "No, I ran away to be an artist." The understanding police officer replied, "Good for you." For many years, Mr. Hodgkin taught art, which he believes is actually "a great trap for an artist as it becomes a substitute life." When he decided to tell art teacher Clifford Ellis that he was going to stop teaching, Mr. Ellis told him, "I know what you're going to say, and I'm amazed it's taken you so long." At age 75, Mr. Hodgkin was working hard on his art, for a practical reason: "Old age." He told reporter Tim Teeman, "I think the time comes when you think, 'Well there's not much time left.' When I was your age, I thought time was endless and suddenly it becomes clear that it's not."[237]

• Claude Monet created a series of paintings with the haystacks of Giverny as their subject. Why did he paint the haystacks over and over? So that he could capture the various kinds of light on them. When he first decided to paint the haystacks, he sent Suzanne Hoschedé, his stepdaughter, to get him two canvases: one for painting the haystacks in direct sunshine, and one for painting the haystacks when a cloud covered the sun. However, he quickly discovered that there were other variations of light that he wanted to paint, and so he kept sending Suzanne to get more canvases. When Suzanne returned with the first two canvases, Monet remembered, "I noticed that the light had changed. I said to [her], 'Would you go back to the house, please, and bring me another canvas?' She brought it to me, but very soon the light had changed again. 'One more!' and, 'One more still!'" Eventually, he was painting on five canvases, moving from one to the other as the light changed.[238]

• Jack Kirby is King of Comics, and his art filled many, many comic books. He was known for working well and quickly, filling page after page with high-quality artwork. However, early in his career Mr. Kirby worked for Victor Fox, a man who paid artists poorly and who wanted profits much more than masterpieces; therefore, Mr. Kirby took shortcuts in his artwork. For example, he would draw a large cloud, which took little work, then add a tiny, quickly drawn airplane to fill a panel of a comic book. One day, he filled an entire panel with the word "Wow." Mr. Fox was puzzled, and he asked Mr. Kirby what was the point of the word "Wow." Mr. Kirby stumbled out an explanation about relating to kids on their level. This satisfied Mr. Fox, and very quickly his other artists started to fill panels with the word

"Wow," knowing — as Mr. Kirby did — that this was a quick way to create a panel.[239]

• The security guards at the National Gallery of Art in Washington, D.C. covet certain rooms to guard. For example, the most coveted rooms are those devoted to the French Impressionists because those works of art are so greatly loved by both the museum visitors and the security guards. For a while, security guards weren't so happy about working in the East Building because those rooms are devoted to 20th-century art, which is more difficult to understand. Sometimes, museum visitors will tell the security guards, "My kid can do better than that!" However, the curators of the 20th-century works of art began to educate the security guards, pointing out that at first people had rejected the French Impressionists and made the same kind of comments about their works of art. After receiving these art lessons, the security guards don't as much mind working in the East Building.[240]

• Famous illustrator Will Eisner remembers the day that he became a professional. He dressed professionally and took his portfolio to a buyer of illustrations. The buyer looked at his illustrated story and said, "This is an awful story! Bah! Stupid faces! Worse drawing! Ugh!" His final comment was, "We don't publish junk." Head hanging down, Mr. Eisner left the buyer's office, and an older man sitting outside the office told him, "So ... your first rejection, eh? There's an old Talmudic saying: 'If you can't sell your wares in this city, go ye to another.'" Then the older man introduced himself to Mr. Eisner and said, "Good luck!" before entering the buyer's office. The man was Ludwig Bemelmans, creator and illustrator of a famous series of children's books starring the character Madeline. Of course, as the world knows, Mr. Eisner persevered and became a renowned illustrator like Mr. Bemelmans.[241]

• While working as an artist at a syndicate called NEA Service, Chic Young received a telephone call that requested that he go to New York and work for King Features Syndicate — with a big raise. He assumed that it was a joke phone call from one of the other employees at NEA Service, and so he replied, "Sorry, but I'm satisfied right here." A few months later, he was fired, and so he went to New York and applied for a job as an artist at King Features Syndicate. One of the first questions that the head of the comic art department, J.D. Gortatowski, asked him was this: "What was the big idea of refusing to come here a couple of months ago when I called you?" United King Syndicate knew a good man when it saw him; Mr. Young created *Blondie* for the syndicate.[242]

• Dean Kamen, inventor of the Segway, learned from his father, who loved his work as an artist and who would sit in front of his drawing board for 12 hours daily. Dean once complained, "Gee, Dad, all the other fathers have time after they come home to play ball or sit around. At the end of the day, you're working." His father replied, "Those fathers are doctors, lawyers and bankers. When they come home, all they want to do is their hobby. My work and my hobby are the same. Find work in something you love and it won't feel like work." The grown-up Dean says, "I listened to him. And I have been fortunate enough to work at something that I love."[243]

• I.T. Frary used to handle publicity for the Cleveland Museum of Art. As a young man new to the staff, he was once hushed in the museum library because he was speaking above a whisper. At night, when the museum was closed and no one was around, Mr. Frary let out a series of loud whoops in the library and felt much better. Other people felt the same way as Mr. Frary about museums — despite being museums, they need not be stuffy. Late at night, when no one else was around, Mr. Frary and a clergyman friend once straddled the museum's marble balustrades and slid down.[244]

• Russ Westover, the cartoonist of the long-ago comic strip *Tillie the Toiler*, got his first drawing job at the *San Francisco Bulletin*. In those days, newspapers used drawings instead of photographs, and one of his first assignments was to go to the mortuary and draw a portrait of a recently drowned person. However, the mortuary was so dark and eerie that Russ left quickly and handed in a drawing of an imaginary recently drowned person.[245]

• Children's book illustrator and author Margot Zemach worked as a movie usherette at the famous Grauman's Chinese Theater when she was young. Unfortunately, she could not see well in the dark and so she was a horrible usherette, often stepping on people's feet and often seating people on top of other people. Fortunately, she got married, started to raise a family, and became a book illustrator — a job she could work at while using one foot to rock a baby bed.[246]

• Some female artists remain creative well into their old age. For example, in 2008 at age 73 Paula Rego was still active and still creating art, pointing out that being creative creates energy: "Even if I'm tired when I start working, by the end I have a lot of energy." She will never willingly retire, saying, "Hopefully [my life] will end at my easel — I'll just fall down sideways. Either that or in a drunken stupor."[247]

• Sculptor Louise Bourgeois worked hard. While on vacation in 1983, without supplies such as clay or wax or Plasticine, she asked her assistant, Jerry Gorovoy, for the shirt he was wearing. She shaped it, sewed it into position, and applied gesso to it. Then she created a marble version of the work of art. The shirt off Mr. Gorovoy's back became the work of art titled *Femme Maison*.[248]

• Thomas Eakins was an instructor at the Pennsylvania Academy of the Fine Arts in the 19th century. He believed that artists ought to have a thorough knowledge of human anatomy, and he was fired after someone walked into his studio and discovered cadavers — which Mr. Eakins had been dissecting.[249]

• American landscape artist George Inness was a perfectionist. Often, he would walk into his studio, look at a painting he had finished the previous day, shake his head, and then paint a new picture on top of the old one.[250]

Appendix A: Book Bibliography

Adler, Bill. *Jewish Wit and Wisdom*. New York: Dell Publishing Co., Inc, 1969.

Alderson, Brian. *Ezra Jack Keats: Artist and Picture-Book Maker*. Gretna, LA: Pelican Publishing Co., Inc., 1994.

The Art of Reading: Forty Illustrators Celebrate RIF's 40th Anniversary. New York: Dutton Books, 2005.

Asch, Frank. *One Man Show*. Katonah, NY: Richard C. Owens Publishers, Inc., 1997.

Auping, Michael. *Jenny Holzer*. New York: Universe Publishing, 1992.

Barter, James. *Artists of the Renaissance*. San Diego, CA: Lucent Books, 1999.

Beardsley, John. *Pablo Picasso*. New York: Harry N. Abrams, Inc., 1991.

Bechdel, Alison. *The Indelible Alison Bechdel: Confessions, Comix, and Miscellaneous Dykes to Watch Out For*. Ithaca, NY: Firebrand Books, 1998.

Bedard, Michael. *William Blake: The Gates of Paradise*. Toronto, Ontario: Tundra Books, 2006.

Belsito, Peter, editor. *Notes from the Pop Underground*. Berkeley, CA: The Last Gasp of San Francisco, 1985.

Berman, Avis. *James McNeill Whistler*. New York: Harry N. Abrams, Inc., 1993.

Bing, Sir Rudolf. *5000 Nights at the Opera*. Garden City, NY: Doubleday and Company, Inc., 1972.

Biracree, Tom. *Grandma Moses*. New York: Chelsea House Publishers, 1989.

Blegvad, Erik. *Erik Blegvad: Self-Portrait*. Reading, MA; Addison-Wesley Publishing Company, Inc., 1979.

Bolden, Tonya. *Wake Up Our Souls: A Celebration of Black America Artists*. New York: Harry N. Abrams, Inc., 2004.

Bryan, Ashley. *Words to My Life's Song*. New York: Atheneum Books for Young Readers, 2009.

Burke, John. *Rogue's Progress: The Fabulous Adventures of Wilson Mizner*. New York: G.P. Putnam's Sons, 1975.

Cain, Michael. *Louise Nevelson*. New York: Chelsea House Publishers, 1989.

Carter, David. *Salvador Dalí*. New York: Chelsea House Publishers, 1995.

Caruso, Dorothy, and Torrance Goddard. *Wings of Song: The Story of Caruso*. New York: Minton, Balch & Company, 1928.

Cossi, Olga. *Edna Hibel: Her Life and Art*. Lowell, MA: Discovery Enterprises, Ltd., 1994.

Crespelle, Jean-Paul, *Monet*. Stamford, CT: Longmeadow Press, 1993.

Cockcroft, James. *Diego Rivera*. New York: Chelsea House Publishers, 1991.

Cruz, Bárbara C. *José Clemente Orozco: Mexican Artist*. Berkeley Heights, NJ: Enslow Publications, Inc., 1998.

Cummings, Pat, compiler and editor. *Talking with Artists*. New York. Bradbury Press, 1992.

Cummings, Pat, compiler and editor. *Talking with Artists, Volume 3*. New York: Simon & Schuster Books for Young Readers, 1999.

Davis, Francis A. *Frank Lloyd Wright: Maverick Architect*. Minneapolis, MN: Lerner Publications Company, 1996.

Deffaw, Chip. *Jazz Veterans: A Portrait Gallery*. Photographs by Nancy Miller Elliott and John & Andreas Johnsen. Fort Bragg, CA: Cypress House Press, 1996.

dePaola, Tomie. *Why?* New York: G.P. Putnam's Sons, 2007.

Diebold, Reinhard, collector and editor. *The Book of Good Deeds: 1914-1918*. Translated by Hellmut and Letitia Lehmann-Haupt. New York: Farrar & Rinehart, 1933.

Doonan, Simon. *Wacky Chicks: Life Lessons from Fearlessly Inappropriate and Fabulously Eccentric Women*. New York: Simon & Schuster, 2003.

Eichenbaum, Rose. *Masters of Movement: Portraits of America's Great Choreographers*. Washington, D.C.: Smithsonian Books, 2004.

Elleman, Barbara. *Tomie dePaola: His Art and His Stories*. New York: G.P. Putnam's Sons, 1999.

Engstead, John. *Star Shots: Fifty Years of Pictures and Stories by One of Hollywood's Greatest Photographers*. New York: E.P. Dutton, 1978.

Eric Carle Museum of Picture Book Art. *Artist to Artist: 23 Major Illustrators Talk to Children About Their Art*. New York: Philomel Books, 2007.

Ericsson, Mary Kentra. *Morrie Turner: Creator of "Wee Pals."* Chicago, IL: Childrens Press, 1986.

Evanier, Mark. *Kirby: King of Comics*. New York: Harry N. Abrams, Inc., 2008.

Evans, Dilys. *Show & Tell: Exploring the Fine Art of Children's Book Illustration*. San Francisco, CA: Chronicle Books, 2008.

Ford, Carin T. *Andy Warhol: Pioneer of Pop Art*. Berkeley Heights, NJ: Enslow Publications, Inc., 2001.

Ford, Corey. *The Time of Laughter*. Boston, MA: Little, Brown and Company, 1967.

Foreman, Michael. *War Boy: A Country Childhood*. New York: Arcade Publishing, Inc., 1990.

Frary, I.T. *At Large in Marble Halls*. Philadelphia, PA: Dorrance & Company, 1959.

Friedman, Kinky. *'Scuse Me While I Whip This Out*. New York: Harper, 2004.

Furst, Herbert. *The New Anecdotes of Painters and Paintings*. London: The Bodley Head, Ltd., 1926.

Garza, Hedda. *Frida Kahlo*. New York: Chelsea House Publishers, 1994.

Gelfand, Ravina, and Letha Patterson. *They Wouldn't Quit: Stories of Handicapped People*. Minneapolis, MN: Lerner Publications Company, 1962.

Gherman, Beverly. *Norman Rockwell: Storyteller with a Brush*. New York: Atheneum Books for Young Readers, 2000.

Gonzales, Doreen. *Diego Rivera: His Art, His Life*. Berkeley Heights, NJ: Enslow Publications, Inc., 1996.

Greenberg, Jan, and Sandra Jordan. *The American Eye: Eleven Artists of the Twentieth Century*. New York: Delacorte Press, 1995.

Greenberg, Jan, and Sandra Jordan. *Runaway Girl: The Artist Louise Bourgeois*. New York: Harry N. Abrams, Inc., 2003.

Greenfield, Howard. *Marc Chagall*. New York: Harry N. Abrams, Inc., 1990.

Head, Edith, and Paddy Calistro. *Edith Head's Hollywood*. New York: E.P. Dutton, Inc., 1983.

Heiderstadt, Dorothy. *Painters of America*. New York: David McKay Company, Inc., 1970.

Heller, Ruth. *Fine Lines*. Katonah, NY: Richard C. Owens Publishers, Inc., 1996.

Henry, Lewis C. *Humorous Anecdotes About Famous People*. Garden City, NY: Halcyon House, 1948.

Isenberg, Barbara. *Conversations with Frank Gehry*. New York: Alfred A. Knopf, 2009.

Isenberg, Barbara. *State of the Arts: California Artists Talk About Their Work*. Chicago, IL: Ivan R. Dee, 2000.

Juno, Andrea, and V. Vale, editors. *Angry Women*. San Francisco, CA: Re/Search Publications, 1999.

Juno, Andrea, and V. Vale, publishers and editors. *Pranks! Devious Deeds and Mischievous Mirth*. San Francisco, CA: Re/Search Publications, 1987.

Kafka, Tina. *Folk Art*. Detroit, MI: Lucent Books, 2008.

Kallen, Stuart A. *Claude Monet*. Detroit, MI: Lucent Books, 2009.

Kamen, Gloria. *Edward Lear: King of Nonsense*. New York: Atheneum, 1990.

Karsh, Yousuf. *Faces of Destiny: Portraits by Karsh*. Chicago, IL: Ziff-Davis Publishing Company, 1946.

Karsh, Yousuf. *Karsh: A Sixty-Year Retrospective*. Boston, MA: Little, Brown and Company, 1996.

Keller, Emily. *Margaret Bourke-White: A Photographer's Life*. Minneapolis, MN: Lerner Publications Company, 1996.

Kent, Allegra. *Once a Dancer …*. New York: St. Martin's Press, 1997.

Kinney, Jack. *Walt Disney and Other Assorted Characters: An Unauthorized Account of the Early Years at Disney's*. New York: Harmony Books, 1988.

Klaiman, Gloria. *Night and Day: The Double Lives of Artists in America*. Westport, CT: Praeger Publishers, 2001.

Koestenbaum, Wayne. *Andy Warhol*. New York: Viking, 2001.

Kostenevich, Albert. *Henri Matisse*. With the collaboration of Lory Frankel. New York: Harry N. Abrams, Inc., Publishers, 1997.

Kovacs, Deborah, and James Preller. *Meet the Authors and Illustrators*. New York: Scholastic, Inc., 1991.

Kovacs, Deborah, and James Preller. *Meet the Authors and Illustrators: Volume Two*. New York: Scholastic, Inc., 1993.

Krull, Kathleen. *Lives of the Artists: Masterpieces, Messes (and What the Neighbors Thought)*. San Diego, CA: Harcourt Brace & Company, 1995.

Levant, Oscar. *A Smattering of Ignorance*. New York: Doubleday, Doran, and Co., 1940.

Lipman, Steve. *Laughter in Hell: The Use of Humor during the Holocaust*. Northvale, NJ: Jason Aronson Inc., 1991.

Loyrette, Henri. *Degas: The Man and His Art*. New York: Abrams, 1993.

Marcovitz, Hal. *Art Conservation*. Detroit, MI: Lucent Books, 2007.

Marcovitz, Hal. *Maurice Sendak*. New York: Chelsea House Publishers, 2006.

Marcus, Leonard S. *Ways of Telling: Conversations on the Art of the Picture Book*. New York: Dutton Children's Books, 2002.

Marshall, Jim. *Not Fade Away: The Rock & Roll Photographs of Jim Marshall*. Boston, MA: Little, Brown and Company, 1997.

Marshall, Jim. *Proof*. "Introduction" by Joel Selvin. San Francisco, CA: Chronicle Books, 2004.

Martin, Rafe. *A Storyteller's Story*. Katonah, NY: Richard C. Owens Publishers, Inc., 1992.

McKown, Robin. *The World of Mary Cassatt*. New York: Dell Publishing Co. Inc., 1972.

McLanathan, Richard. *Michelangelo*. New York: Harry N. Abrams, Publishers, 1993.

Meyer, Susan E. *Edgar Degas*. New York: Harry N. Abrams, Inc., 1994.

Meyer, Susan E. *Mary Cassatt*. New York: Harry N. Abrams, Inc., 1990.

Miller, John, editor. *Legends: Women Who Have Changed the World*. Novato, CA: New World Books, 1998.

Mostel, Kate, and Madeline Gilford. *170 Years of Show Business*. With Jack Gilford and Zero Mostel. New York: Random House, 1978.

Norkin, Sam. *Drawings, Stories: Theater, Opera, Ballet, Movies.* Portsmouth, NH: Heinemann, 1994.

Pinet, Hélène. *Rodin: The Hands of Genius.* Trans. Caroline Palmer. New York: Harry N. Abrams, Inc., 1992.

Rayfield, Susan. *Pierre-Auguste Renoir.* New York: Harry N. Abrams, Publishers, 1998.

Rayner, William P. *Wise Women.* New York: St. Martin's Press, 1983.

Reidelbach, Maria. *Completely MAD: A History of the Comic Book and Magazine.* Boston, MA: Little, Brown and Company, 1991.

Richardson, Martha. *Francisco Goya.* New York: Chelsea House Publishers, 1994.

Robbins, Trina. *From Girls to Grrrls.* San Francisco, CA: Chronicle Books, 1999.

Roberts, Russell. *Rulers of Ancient Egypt.* San Diego, CA: Lucent Books, 1999.

Rogers, Fred. *You Are Special.* New York: Viking, 1994.

Rubin, Susan Goldman. *Delicious: The Life & Art of Wayne Thiebaud.* San Francisco, CA: Chronicle Books, 2007.

Rubin, Susan Goldman. *Frank Lloyd Wright.* New York: Harry N. Abrams, Inc., 1994.

Ryan, Jay. *100 Posters, 134 Squirrels: A Decade of Hot Dogs, Large Mammals, and Independent Rock.* Chicago, IL: Punk Planet Books, 2005.

Schultz, Diana, editor. *AutobioGraphix.* Milwaukie, OR: Dark Horse Books, 2003.

Schwartz, Gary. *Rembrandt.* New York: Harry N. Abrams, 1992.

Selfridge, John W. *Pablo Picasso.* New York: Chelsea House Publishers, 1994.

Sheridan, Martin. *Comics and Their Creators: Life Stories of American Cartoonists.* Westport, CT: Hyperion Press, Inc., 1977.

Slezak, Leo. *Song of Motley.* New York: Arno Press, 1977.

Smaridge, Norah. *Famous Literary Teams for Young People.* New York: Dodd, Mead and Company, 1977.

Sobol, Donald J. *Encyclopedia Brown's Book of Wacky Cars.* New York: William Morrow and Company, Inc., 1987.

Soyer, Raphael. *A Painter's Pilgrimage: An Account of a Journey with Drawings by the Author.* New York: Crown Publishers, Inc., 1962.

Sufrin, Mark, *George Catlin: Painter of the Indian West.* New York: Atheneum, 1991.

Swisher, Clarice. *Pablo Picasso.* San Diego, CA: Lucent Books, 1995.

Theroux, Alexander. *The Enigma of Al Capp.* Seattle, WA: Fantagraphics Books, 1999.

Theroux, Alexander. *The Strange Case of Edward Gorey.* Seattle, WA: Fantagraphics Books, 2000.

Thomson, Peggy. *The Nine-Ton Cat: Behind the Scenes at an Art Museum*. With Barbara Moore. Edited by Carol Eron. Boston, MA: Houghton Mifflin Company, 1997.

Troy, Con. *Laugh with Hugh Troy, World's Greatest Practical Joker*. Wyomissing, PA: Trojan Books, 1983.

Turner, Alwyn W. *Halfway to Paradise: The Birth of British Rock*. Photographs by Harry Hammond from the V&A Collection. London: V&A Publishing, 2008.

Uecker, Bob, and Mickey Herskowitz. *Catcher in the Wry*. New York: G.P. Putnam's Sons, 1982.

Von Hohenberg, Christophe, photographer. *Andy Warhol: The Day the Factory Died*. Text by Charlie Schieps. New York: Empire Editions, 2006.

Waldron, Ann. *Claude Monet*. New York: Harry N. Abrams, Inc., 1991.

Warren, Roz, editor. *Dyke Strippers: Lesbian Cartoonists A to Z*. Pittsburgh, PA: Cleis Press, Inc., 1995.

Wertheim, Lucy Carrington. *Adventure in Art*. London: Nicholson and Watson, 1947.

Whistler, James Abbott McNeill. *The Gentle Art of Making Enemies*. New York: Dover Publications, Inc., 1967.

Young, Richard. *Shooting Stars*. London: Metro Publishing, Ltd., 2004.

Zemach, Margot. *Self-Portrait: Margot Zemach*. Reading, MA: Addison-Wesley Company, Inc., 1978.

Zuckerman, Andrew. *Wisdom*. Edited by Alex Vlack. New York: Harry N. Abrams, Inc., 2008.

Appendix B: About the Author

It was a dark and stormy night. Suddenly a cry rang out, and on a hot summer night in 1954, Josephine, wife of Carl Bruce, gave birth to a boy — me. Unfortunately, this young married couple allowed Reuben Saturday, Josephine's brother, to name their first-born. Reuben, aka "The Joker," decided that Bruce was a nice name, so he decided to name me Bruce Bruce. I have gone by my middle name — David — ever since.

Being named Bruce David Bruce hasn't been all bad. Bank tellers remember me very quickly, so I don't often have to show an ID. It can be fun in charades, also. When I was a counselor as a teenager at Camp Echoing Hills in Warsaw, Ohio, a fellow counselor gave the signs for "sounds like" and "two words," then she pointed to a bruise on her leg twice. Bruise Bruise? Oh yeah, Bruce Bruce is the answer!

Uncle Reuben, by the way, gave me a haircut when I was in kindergarten. He cut my hair short and shaved a small bald spot on the back of my head. My mother wouldn't let me go to school until the bald spot grew out again.

Of all my brothers and sisters (six in all), I am the only transplant to Athens, Ohio. I was born in Newark, Ohio, and have lived all around Southeastern Ohio. However, I moved to Athens to go to Ohio University and have never left.

At Ohio U, I never could make up my mind whether to major in English or Philosophy, so I got a bachelor's degree with a double major in both areas, then I added a Master of Arts degree in English and a Master of Arts degree in Philosophy. Yes, I have my MAMA degree.

Currently, and for a long time to come (I eat fruits and veggies), I am spending my retirement writing books such as *Nadia Comaneci: Perfect 10*, *The Funniest People in Comedy*, *Homer's* Iliad: *A Retelling in Prose*, and *William Shakespeare's* Hamlet: *A Retelling in Prose*.

By the way, my sister Brenda Kennedy writes romances such as *A New Beginning* and *Shattered Dreams*.

Appendix C: Some Books by David Bruce

Anecdote Collections

250 Anecdotes About Opera

250 Anecdotes About Religion

250 Anecdotes About Religion: Volume 2

250 Music Anecdotes

Be a Work of Art: 250 Anecdotes and Stories

The Coolest People in Art: 250 Anecdotes

The Coolest People in the Arts: 250 Anecdotes

The Coolest People in Books: 250 Anecdotes

The Coolest People in Comedy: 250 Anecdotes

Create, Then Take a Break: 250 Anecdotes

Don't Fear the Reaper: 250 Anecdotes

The Funniest People in Art: 250 Anecdotes

The Funniest People in Books: 250 Anecdotes

The Funniest People in Books, Volume 2: 250 Anecdotes

The Funniest People in Books, Volume 3: 250 Anecdotes

The Funniest People in Comedy: 250 Anecdotes

The Funniest People in Dance: 250 Anecdotes

The Funniest People in Families: 250 Anecdotes

The Funniest People in Families, Volume 2: 250 Anecdotes

The Funniest People in Families, Volume 3: 250 Anecdotes

The Funniest People in Families, Volume 4: 250 Anecdotes

The Funniest People in Families, Volume 5: 250 Anecdotes

The Funniest People in Families, Volume 6: 250 Anecdotes

The Funniest People in Movies: 250 Anecdotes

The Funniest People in Music: 250 Anecdotes

The Funniest People in Music, Volume 2: 250 Anecdotes

The Funniest People in Music, Volume 3: 250 Anecdotes

The Funniest People in Neighborhoods: 250 Anecdotes

The Funniest People in Relationships: 250 Anecdotes

The Funniest People in Sports: 250 Anecdotes

The Funniest People in Sports, Volume 2: 250 Anecdotes

The Funniest People in Television and Radio: 250 Anecdotes

The Funniest People in Theater: 250 Anecdotes

The Funniest People Who Live Life: 250 Anecdotes

The Funniest People Who Live Life, Volume 2: 250 Anecdotes

The Kindest People Who Do Good Deeds, Volume 1: 250 Anecdotes

The Kindest People Who Do Good Deeds, Volume 2: 250 Anecdotes

Maximum Cool: 250 Anecdotes

The Most Interesting People in Movies: 250 Anecdotes

The Most Interesting People in Politics and History: 250 Anecdotes

The Most Interesting People in Politics and History, Volume 2: 250 Anecdotes

The Most Interesting People in Politics and History, Volume 3: 250 Anecdotes

The Most Interesting People in Religion: 250 Anecdotes

The Most Interesting People in Sports: 250 Anecdotes

The Most Interesting People Who Live Life: 250 Anecdotes

The Most Interesting People Who Live Life, Volume 2: 250 Anecdotes

Reality is Fabulous: 250 Anecdotes and Stories

Resist Psychic Death: 250 Anecdotes

Seize the Day: 250 Anecdotes and Stories

[1] Source: Jonathan Jones, "A gallery of ghosts." *The Guardian*. 25 October 2007 <http://www.guardian.co.uk/g2/story/0,,2198435,00.html>.

[2] Source: Lauren Collins, "Banksy Was Here: The invisible man of graffiti art." *The New Yorker*. 14 May 2007 <http://www.newyorker.com/reporting/2007/05/14/070514fa_fact_collins>.

[3] Source: Simon Doonan, *Wacky Chicks*, p. 218.

[4] Source: Martha Richardson, *Francisco Goya*, pp. 16, 83.

[5] Source: Germaine Greer, "Instead of spending a fortune getting rid of graffiti, why don't we just give it marks out of 10?" *The Guardian*. 24 September 2007 <http://arts.guardian.co.uk/art/visualart/story/0,,2175701,00.html>.

[6] Source: "Gioia to graduates: 'Trade easy pleasures for more complex and challenging ones.'" *Stanford Report*. 17 June 2007 <http://news-service.stanford.edu/news/2007/june20/gradtrans-062007.html>.

[7] Source: Richard Young, *Shooting Stars*, pp. 162-163.

[8] Source: Con Troy, *Laugh with Hugh Troy*, pp. 149-153.

[9] Source: Germaine Greer, "Why do so many female artists put themselves in their work? — often with no clothes on?" *The Guardian*. 28 January 2008 <http://www.guardian.co.uk/g2/story/0,,2247942,00.html>.

[10] Source: David Patrick Stearns, "Laurie Anderson: Eclectic storyteller who keeps her cool." *The Philadelphia Inquirer*. 14 July 2010 <http://www.popmatters.com/pm/article/128259-laurie-anderson-eclectic-storyteller-who-keeps-her-cool/>.

[11] Source: Christophe Von Hohenberg, photographer, *Andy Warhol: The Day the Factory Died*, unnumbered pages.

[12] Source: Deborah Kovacs and James Preller, *Meet the Authors and Illustrators: Volume Two*, p. 79.

[13] Source: Andrea Juno and V. Vale, publishers and editors, *Pranks! Devious Deeds and Mischievous Mirth*, p. 110.

[14] Source: *The Art of Reading: Forty Illustrators Celebrate RIF's 40th Anniversary*, pp. 30-31.

[15] Source: Kevin Berger, "When Patti Smith and Robert Mapplethorpe were 'Just Kids.'" *Los Angeles Times.* 17 January 2010 <http://www.latimes.com/entertainment/news/la-ca-patti-smith17-2010jan17,0,1698405,full.story>.

[16]Source: Pat Cummings, compiler and editor, *Talking with Artists, Volume 3,* p. 52.

[17] Source: John Engstead, *Star Shots: Fifty Years of Pictures and Stories by One of Hollywood's Greatest Photographers,* p. 200.

[18] Source: Norah Smaridge, *Famous Literary Teams for Young People,* pp. 131, 135-136.

[19] Source: John W. Selfridge, *Pablo Picasso,* p. 23.

[20]Source: Alfred Werner, "Introduction" to James Abbott McNeill Whistler's *The Gentle Art of Making Enemies,* p. viii.

[21] Source: Roger Ebert, "Books do furnish a life." *Roger Ebert's Journal.* 5 October 2009 <http://blogs.suntimes.com/ebert/2009/10/books_do_furnish_a_life.html>.

[22] Source: Rafe Martin, *A Storyteller's Story,* pp. 16-17, 25.

[23] Source: Barbara Elleman, *Tomie dePaola: His Art and His Stories,* pp. 97-98.

[24] Source: Alexander Theroux, *The Strange Case of Edward Gorey,* p. 11.

[25] Source: Eric Carle Museum of Picture Book Art, *Artist to Artist: 23 Major Illustrators Talk to Children About Their Art,* p. 82.

[26]Source: Brian Alderson, *Ezra Jack Keats: Artist and Picture-Book Maker,* p. 55.

[27] Source: Michael Auping, *Jenny Holzer,* pp. 10, 12, 26, 28, 71, 78, 107.

[28]Source: Roz Warren, editor, *Dyke Strippers: Lesbian Cartoonists A to Z,* pp. 41-42.

[29]Source: Bárbara C. Cruz, *José Clemente Orozco: Mexican Artist,* pp. 31-32.

[30]Source: Doreen Gonzales, *Diego Rivera: His Art, His Life,* pp. 58, 60.

[31]Source: Steve Lipman, *Laughter in Hell,* pp. 84-85.

[32] Source: Kelly Virella, "The Strange Drawings of Brian Brooks." *East Bay Express.* 31 October 2007 <http://news.eastbayexpress.com/2007-10-31/news/the-strange-drawings-of-brian-brooks/>.

[33] Source: Dilys Evans, *Show & Tell: Exploring the Fine Art of Children's Book Illustration,* pp. 90, 95.

[34] Source: *The Art of Reading: Forty Illustrators Celebrate RIF's 40th Anniversary*, pp. 38-39.

[35] Source: Pat Cummings, compiler and editor, *Talking with Artists*, p. 17.

[36] Source: Tomie dePaola, *Why?*, pp. 52-60.

[37] Source: Tonya Bolden, *Wake Up Our Souls*, p. 50.

[38] Source: Hal Marcovitz, *Maurice Sendak*, p. 105.

[39] Source: Norah Smaridge, *Famous Literary Teams for Young People*, pp. 60-61.

[40] Source: Dominick A. Miserandino, "Interview with Bob Weber, cartoonist." <http://thecelebritycafe.com/interviews/bob_weber.html>. Accessed 10 April 2008.

[41] Source: Emily Keller, *Margaret Bourke-White: A Photographer's Life*, p. 18.

[42] Source: Pat Cummings, compiler and editor, *Talking with Artists, Volume 3*, p. 22.

[43] Source: David Carter, *Salvador Dalí*, p. 26.

[44] Source: Fred Rogers, *You Are Special*, p. 61.

[45] Source: Wayne Koestenbaum, *Andy Warhol*, pp. 114, 150, 171-72, 176, 213.

[46] Source: Ravina Gelfand and Letha Patterson, *They Wouldn't Quit: Stories of Handicapped People*, pp. 33-36.

[47] Source: Susan Rayfield, *Pierre-Auguste Renoir*, p. 48.

[48] Source: Olga Cossi, *Edna Hibel: Her Life and Art*, p. 94.

[49] Source: Kathleen Krull, *Lives of the Artists*, p. 78.

[50] Source: Albert Kostenevich, *Henri Matisse*, pp. 31-32, 39, 52.

[51] Source: John Burke, *Rogue's Progress: The Fabulous Adventures of Wilson Mizner*, pp. 99-100.

[52] Source: Raphael Soyer, *A Painter's Pilgrimage: An Account of a Journey with Drawings by the Author*, p. 39.

[53] Source: Jonathan Ross, "Jonathan Ross meets Jim Steranko, his comic-book hero." *The Guardian*. 21 July 2010 <http://www.guardian.co.uk/books/2010/jul/21/jim-steranko-comics-jonathan-ross>.

[54] Source: Trina Robbins, *From Girls to Grrrls*, pp. 128-130.

[55] Source: "Oh boy, Charlie Brown: Matt Groening and Jonathan Franzen pay tribute to 'Peanuts.'" *The Guardian*. 11 October 2008 <http://www.guardian.co.uk/books/2008/oct/11/peanuts-matt-groening-jonathan-franzen>.

[56] Source: Brent Hartinger, "The Cartoon Closet." AfterElton. 18 May 2008 <http://www.afterelton.com/Print/2008/5/cartooncloset>.

[57] Source: Mark Evanier, *Kirby: King of Comics*, p. 215.

[58] Source: Barbara Isenberg, *Conversations with Frank Gehry*, pp. 189-195.

[59] Source: "35 Greatest Works of Reverse Graffiti." 21 August 2008 <http://www.environmentalgraffiti.com/featured/35-greatest-works-of-reverse-graffiti/1949>. Also: <http://www.reversegraffitiproject.com/index.html>. So to <Youtube.com> and search for "reverse graffiti."

[60] Source: Jim Marshall, *Not Fade Away: The Rock & Roll Photographs of Jim Marshall*, p. 129. This anecdote comes from the Afterword: "Still Crazy After All These Years," by Jon Bowernaster.

[61] Source: Mark Sufrin, *George Catlin: Painter of the Indian West*, p. 103.

[62] Source: James Abbott McNeill Whistler, *The Gentle Art of Making Enemies*, p. 71.

[63] Source: Dorothy Heiderstadt, *Painters of America*, p. 40.

[64] Source: Hélène Pinet, *Rodin: The Hands of Genius*, pp. 18, 26-27.

[65] Source: Wayne Koestenbaum, *Andy Warhol*, pp. 34, 59-60, 64.

[66] Source: Leo Slezak, *Song of Motley*, pp. 293-294.

[67] Source: Martha Richardson, *Francisco Goya*, pp. 15, 19-21.

[68] Source: Raphael Soyer, *A Painter's Pilgrimage: An Account of a Journey with Drawings by the Author*, pp. 58-59.

[69] Source: Kinky Friedman, *'Scuse Me While I Whip This Out*, p. 187.

[70] Source: Jessica Hopper, "Grief Made Graphic." *The Chicago Reader*. 7 September 2007 <http://www.chicagoreader.com/features/stories/andersnilsen/>.

[71] Source: Ed Potton, "Brian Blessed, actor and adventurer, stars in *Peter and the Wolf*." 22 March 2008 <http://entertainment.timesonline.co.uk/tol/arts_and_entertainment/stage/theatre/article3576027.ece>.

[72] Source: Lewis C. Henry, *Humorous Anecdotes About Famous People*, p. 28.

[73] Source: Susan Rayfield, *Pierre-Auguste Renoir*, pp. 13, 16.

[74] Source: Clarice Swisher, *Pablo Picasso*, pp. 44-45.

[75]Source: Simon Doonan, *Wacky Chicks*, p. 102.

[76] Source: Alexander Theroux, *The Strange Case of Edward Gorey*, p. 49.

[77] Source: Allegra Kent, *Once a Dancer ...*, p. 51.

[78] Source: Rose Eichenbaum, *Masters of Movement: Portraits of America's Great Choreographers*, p. 31.

[79] Source: Stuart A. Kallen, *Claude Monet*, pp. 39, 71-72.

[80]Source: Bárbara C. Cruz, *José Clemente Orozco: Mexican Artist*, p. 101.

[81] Source: Jean-Paul Crespelle, *Monet*, p. 41.

[82]Source: Leo Slezak, *Song of Motley*, p. 293.

[83] Source: David Carter, *Salvador Dalí*, pp. 14-17, 35-38.

[84] Source: Jay Ryan, *100 Posters, 134 Squirrels: A Decade of Hot Dogs, Large Mammals, and Independent Rock*, pp. 65, 100, 109, 112.

[85] Source: Frank Asch, *One Man Show*, pp. 6, 15, 28-31.

[86] Source: Nicole Jackson, "The teacher who inspired me." *The Guardian*. 19 January 2010 <http://www.guardian.co.uk/education/2010/jan/19/teacher-inspired-me>.

[87] Source: Barbara Isenberg, *Conversations with Frank Gehry*, p. 21.

[88] Source: Beverly Gherman, *Norman Rockwell: Storyteller with a Brush*, pp. 35, 38.

[89] Source: Dilys Evans, *Show & Tell: Exploring the Fine Art of Children's Book Illustration*, p. 121.

[90] Source: Peggy Thomson, *The Nine-Ton Cat: Behind the Scenes at an Art Museum*, pp. 82-83.

[91] Source: Ruth Heller, *Fine Lines*, pp. 20-21.

[92]Source: Jan Greenberg and Sandra Jordan, *Runaway Girl: The Artist Louise Bourgeois*, p. 30.

[93]Source: Francis A. Davis, *Frank Lloyd Wright: Maverick Architect*, pp. 91-92.

[94]Source: Avis Berman, *James McNeill Whistler*, p. 19.

[95]Source: Jan Greenberg and Sandra Jordan, *The American Eye: Eleven Artists of the Twentieth Century*, p. 71.

[96] Source: Fred Rogers, *You Are Special*, pp. 86-87.

[97]Source: Herbert Furst, *The New Anecdotes of Painters and Paintings*, p. 9.

[98]Source: Deborah Kovacs and James Preller, *Meet the Authors and Illustrators*, p. 17.

[99] Source: Edmund White, "The Beats: Pictures of a Legend." *The New York Review of Books*. 22 July 2010 <http://www.nybooks.com/blogs/nyrblog/2010/jul/22/beats-pictures-legend/>.

[100] Source: Yousuf Karsh, *Karsh: A Sixty-Year Retrospective*, p. 155.

[101]Source: Jack Kinney, *Walt Disney and Other Assorted Characters*, p. 149.

[102] Source: Tom Shone, The *Sunday Times* Review of "*Schulz and Peanuts: A Biography* by David Michaelis." *The Times*. 19 October 2008 <http://entertainment.timesonline.co.uk/tol/arts_and_entertainment/books/non-fiction/article4954796.ece>.

[103]Source: Avis Berman, *James McNeill Whistler*, p. 55.

[104] Source: Susan Goldman Rubin, *Delicious: The Life & Art of Wayne Thiebaud*, pp. 53-55.

[105] Source: James Cockcroft, *Diego Rivera*, p. 66.

[106] Source: Barbara Isenberg, *State of the Arts: California Artists Talk About Their Work*, p. 5.

[107]Source: Michael Cain, *Louise Nevelson*, pp. 61, 66.

[108]Source: Sam Norkin, *Drawings, Stories*, pp. 188-189.

[109]Source: Corey Ford, *The Time of Laughter*, p. 129.

[110]Source: Roz Warren, editor, *Dyke Strippers: Lesbian Cartoonists A to Z*, p. 198.

[111]Source: Alison Bechdel, *The Indelible Alison Bechdel*, p. 213.

[112] Source: Diane Root, "Food: Eat, Memory." *The New York Times*. 17 October 2008 <http://www.nytimes.com/2008/10/19/magazine/19food-t.html?_r=1&oref=slogin>.

[113] Source: Richard McLanathan, *Peter Paul Rubens*, pp. 27-29.

[114] Source: Ashley Bryan, *Words to My Life's Song*, pp. 37, 41.

[115] Source: Chip Deffaw, *Jazz Veterans: A Portrait Gallery*, p. ix.

[116] Source: Lucy Carrington Wertheim, *Adventure in Art*, p. 37.

[117]Source: Sir Rudolf Bing, *5000 Nights at the Opera*, pp. 302-303.

[118] Source: Dorothy Caruso and Torrance Goddard, *Wings of Song: The Story of Caruso*, pp. 81-83.

[119] Source: Ashley Bryan, *Words to My Life's Song*, pp. 47, 50, 56, back cover.

[120] Source: Reinhard Diebold, collector and editor, *The Book of Good Deeds: 1914-1918*, pp. 110-111.

[121] Source: Richard McLanathan, *Peter Paul Rubens*, p. 47.

[122] Source: Barbara Elleman, *Tomie dePaola: His Art and His Stories*, p. 145.

[123] Source: Michael Foreman, *War Boy: A Country Childhood*, p. 65.

[124] Source: Hal Marcovitz, *Art Conservation*, p. 11.

[125]Source: Sam Norkin, *Drawings, Stories*, p. 306.

[126] Source: Andrew Zuckerman, *Wisdom*, p. 194.

[127] Source: Jean-Paul Crespelle, *Monet*, p. 118.

[128] Source: Tina Kafka, *Folk Art*, pp. 14, 69-71. Also: "Sadako Sasaki." Wikipedia. Accessed 11 December 2010.

[129] Source: Susan Goldman Rubin, *Delicious: The Life & Art of Wayne Thiebaud*, p. 25.

[130]Source: Howard Greenfield, *Marc Chagall*, p. 62.

[131]Source: Mary Kentra Ericsson, *Morrie Turner: Creator of "Wee Pals,"* p. 66.

[132] Source: Leonard S. Marcus, *Ways of Telling: Conversations on the Art of the Picture Book*, pp. 167, 229.

[133] Source: Deborah Kovacs and James Preller, *Meet the Authors and Illustrators: Volume Two*, p. 27.

[134] Source: Valerie Grove, "I appreciate your gift more than I can say." *The Times*. 27 December 2007 <http://women.timesonline.co.uk/tol/life_and_style/women/the_way_we_live/article3097017.ece>.

[135] Source: Maria Reidelbach, *Completely MAD*, p. 114.

[136]Source: Carin T. Ford, *Andy Warhol: Pioneer of Pop Art*, pp. 13, 46-47, 53, 62-64.

[137]Source: Tom Biracree, *Grandma Moses*, pp. 86, 88.

[138]Source: Michael Cain, *Louise Nevelson*, p. 105.

[139] Source: Edith Head and Paddy Calistro, *Edith Head's Hollywood*, pp. viii, 6-7, 11-12.

[140] Source: Susan Goldman Rubin, *Frank Lloyd Wright*, pp. 53, 59, 81.

[141] Source: Luke Harding, "My grandad, the clown." *The Guardian*. 10 February 2009 <http://www.guardian.co.uk/artanddesign/2009/feb/10/tate-modern-modernism>.

[142] Source: Gloria Kamen, *Edward Lear: King of Nonsense*, pp. 51-52.

[143] Source: Jim Hightower, "COWBOY GEORGE, THE HORSE THIEF." 8 February 2008 <http://www.jimhightower.com/node/6332>. Also: "The Inspiration." 26 January 2008 <http://blogd.com/wp/index.php/archives/3271>.

[144] Source: Hal Marcovitz, *Art Conservation*, p. 76.

[145] Source: Yousuf Karsh, *Karsh: A Sixty-Year Retrospective*, p. 125.

[146] Source: Peter Belsito, editor, *Notes from the Pop Underground*, p. 58.

[147] Source: Susan E. Meyer, *Edgar Degas*, p. 44.

[148] Source: William P. Rayner, *Wise Women*, pp. 2-3.

[149] Source: Olga Cossi, *Edna Hibel: Her Life and Art*, p. 28.

[150] Source: Henri Loyrette, *Degas: The Man and His Art*, p. 158.

[151] Source: Oscar Levant, *A Smattering of Ignorance*, pp. 82-83.

[152] Source: Bob Uecker and Mickey Herskowitz, *Catcher in the Wry*, pp. 183-184.

[153] Source: Susan E. Meyer, *Edgar Degas*, p. 47.

[154] Source: Ann Waldron, *Claude Monet*, p. 17.

[155] Source: James Bone, "How a 'skip-rat' managed to turn rubbish into a $1m work of art." *The Times*. 24 October 2007 <http://entertainment.timesonline.co.uk/tol/arts_and_entertainment/visual_arts/article2726631.ece>.

[156] Source: Michael Bedard, *William Blake: The Gates of Paradise*, pp. 148-149.

[157] Source: Gary Schwartz, *Rembrandt*, pp. 29, 74.

[158] Source: Travis R. Wright, "Banksy bombs Detroit." *Metro Times*. 19 May 2010 http://www.metrotimes.com/arts/story.asp?id=15063.

[159] Source: Ed Pilkington, "Garry Trudeau: 'Doonesbury Quickly Became a Cause of Trouble.'" *The Guardian*. 26 October 2010 <http://www.guardian.co.uk/books/2010/oct/26/garry-trudeau-doonesbury-40>.

[160]Source: Tom Biracree, *Grandma Moses*, pp. 13-14, 61-62, 84.

[161] Source: Waldemar Januszczak, "Time for a cull in the art world." *Sunday Times*. 11 January 2009 <http://entertainment.timesonline.co.uk/tol/arts_and_entertainment/visual_arts/article5475054.ece>.

[162]Source: Kate Mostel and Madeline Gilford, *170 Years of Show Business*, pp. 46-47.

[163] Source: Alwyn W. Turner, *Halfway to Paradise: The Birth of British Rock*, p. 13.

[164] Source: Mark Rappolt, "Ellsworth Kelly is the king of colour." *The Times*. 11 June 2008 <http://entertainment.timesonline.co.uk/tol/arts_and_entertainment/visual_arts/article4105667.ece>.

[165]Source: Bill Adler, *Jewish Wit and Wisdom*, pp. 17-18.

[166] Source: Chip Deffaw, *Jazz Veterans: A Portrait Gallery*, pp. x-xi.

[167]Source: Lewis C. Henry, *Humorous Anecdotes About Famous People*, p. 19.

[168]Source: Herbert Furst, *The New Anecdotes of Painters and Paintings*, pp. 47-48.

[169] Source: Trina Robbins, *From Girls to Grrrls*, p.134.

[170] Source: Leonard S. Marcus, *Ways of Telling: Conversations on the Art of the Picture Book*, pp. 192, 198, 217.

[171] Source: Margot Zemach, *Self-Portrait: Margot Zemach*, pp. 12-13.

[172] Source: Hal Marcovitz, *Maurice Sendak*, p. 21.

[173] Source: Gloria Klaiman, *Night and Day: The Double Lives of Artists in America*, p. 66.

[174] Source: Eric Carle Museum of Picture Book Art, *Artist to Artist: 23 Major Illustrators Talk to Children About Their Art*, p. 38.

[175] Source: Nicholas Serota, "I work in waves." *The Guardian*. 3 June 2008 <http://arts.guardian.co.uk/art/visualart/story/0,,2283478,00.html>.

[176] Source: Will Harris, "A Chat with David Morse." Bullz-eye.com. 9 June 2008 <http://www.bullz-eye.com/television/interviews/2008/david_morse.htm>.

[177] Source: John Engstead, *Star Shots: Fifty Years of Pictures and Stories by One of Hollywood's Greatest Photographers*, p. 190.

[178] Source: Erik Blegvad, *Erik Blegvad: Self-Portrait*, pp. 14, 18, 23.

[179] Source: Mark Sufrin, *George Catlin: Painter of the Indian West*, pp. 47, 51, 99-101.

[180] Source: Kathleen Krull, *Lives of the Artists*, pp. 33, 35.

[181] Source: Susan E. Meyer, *Mary Cassatt*, p. 22.

[182] Source: Barbara Isenberg, *State of the Arts: California Artists Talk About Their Work*, pp. 68-69.

[183] Source: Howard Greenfield, *Marc Chagall*, p. 37.

[184] Source: Richard McLanathan, *Michelangelo*, p. 68.

[185] Source: Vic Leighliter, "Letter to the Editor." *The Athens News*. 31 December 2009 <http://www.athensnews.com/editorial/letters/29981-another-athenian-and-figure-in-the-local-arts-scene-becomes-a-centurion>.

[186] Source: Gloria Klaiman, *Night and Day: The Double Lives of Artists in America*, pp. 79-80.

[187] Source: Jan Greenberg and Sandra Jordan, *The American Eye: Eleven Artists of the Twentieth Century*, pp. 9-10.

[188] Source: Roger Ebert, "The Agony of the Body Artist." *Roger Ebert's Journal*. 14 October 2009 <http://blogs.suntimes.com/ebert/2009/10/the_agony_of_the_body_artist.html>.

[189] Source: Nick Claussen, "Student performance artists use Athens area as their canvas." *The Athens News*. 9 July 2007 <http://www.athensnews.com/index.php?action=viewarticle§ion=news&story_id=28742>.

[190] Source: Andrea Juno and V. Vale, editors, *Angry Women*, pp. 187-189.

[191] Source: Geoff Boucher, "Leonard Nimoy in search of human life forms through photography." *Los Angeles Times*. 30 October 2009 <http://latimesblogs.latimes.com/herocomplex/2009/10/leonard-nimoy-searches-for-human-life-forms-through-photography.html>. Check out <http://www.leonardnimoyphotography.com/index.htm>.

[192] Source: Yousuf Karsh, *Faces of Destiny: Portraits by Karsh*, pp. 130-131.

[193] Source: Carol Strickland, "Karsh's Art — Iconic Yet Intimate." *Christian Science Monitor*. 3 October 2008 <http://www.csmonitor.com/2008/1003/p13s01-algn.html>.

[194] Source: Jim Marshall, *Proof*, unnumbered pages.

[195] Source: Rose Eichenbaum, *Masters of Movement: Portraits of America's Great Choreographers*, p. 139.

[196] Source: Yousuf Karsh, *Faces of Destiny: Portraits by Karsh*, pp. 120-121.

[197] Source: Jim Marshall, *Not Fade Away: The Rock & Roll Photographs of Jim Marshall*, p. 4.

[198] Source: Tom Robbins, "Fred W. McDarrah, 1926-2007." *The Village Voice*. 6 November 2007 <http://www.villagevoice.com/news/0745,robbins,78255,2.html>. This article includes reminiscences of Mr. McDarrah by Wayne Barrett and J. Hoberman.

[199] Source: Lucy Carrington Wertheim, *Adventure in Art*, p. 3.

[200] Source: Pat Cummings, compiler and editor, *Talking with Artists*, pp. 68-69.

[201] Source: Andrea Juno and V. Vale, publishers and editors, *Pranks! Devious Deeds and Mischievous Mirth*, pp. 28-32.

[202] Source: Hedda Garza, *Frida Kahlo*, pp. 30, 41.

[203] Source: James Barter, *Artists of the Renaissance*, pp. 19-20.

[204] Source: Con Troy, *Laugh with Hugh Troy*, pp. 20-21.

[205] Source: John Miller, editor, *Legends: Women Who Have Changed the World*, pp. 16-17.

[206] Source: James Cockcroft, *Diego Rivera*, pp. 26, 74, 86.

[207] Source: Tonya Bolden, *Wake Up Our Souls*, pp. 45-46.

[208] Source: Susan E. Meyer, *Mary Cassatt*, pp. 54, 63.

[209] Source: Kirsten Akens, "Pakistani Cartoonist Nigar Nazar Spreads a Female-Focused Message." *Colorado Springs Independent*. 8 October 2009 <http://www.csindy.com/colorado/gogi-power/Content?oid=1459668>.

[210] Source: Edith Head and Paddy Calistro, *Edith Head's Hollywood*, p. 93.

[211] Source: John Beardsley, *Pablo Picasso*, pp. 16, 22, 30.

[212] Source: Allegra Kent, *Once a Dancer...*, p. 161.

[213] Source: Doreen Gonzales, *Diego Rivera: His Art, His Life*, p. 109.

[214] Source: Christophe Von Hohenberg, photographer, *Andy Warhol: The Day the Factory Died*, unnumbered pages.

[215] Source: Beverly Gherman, *Norman Rockwell: Storyteller with a Brush*, p. 11.

[216] Source: Susan Goldman Rubin, *Frank Lloyd Wright*, p. 81.

[217] Source: Francis A. Davis, *Frank Lloyd Wright: Maverick Architect*, pp. 72, 109.

[218] Source: Alexander Theroux, *The Enigma of Al Capp*, p. 21.

[219] Source: Emily Keller, *Margaret Bourke-White: A Photographer's Life*, pp. 35-36.

[220] Source: Herbert Furst, *The New Anecdotes of Painters and Paintings*, p. 63.

[221] Source: Ann Waldron, *Claude Monet*, p. 33.

[222] Source: Carin T. Ford, *Andy Warhol: Pioneer of Pop Art*, pp. 82-83.

[223] Source: Russell Roberts, *Rulers of Ancient Egypt*, pp. 24ff.

[224] Source: Richard Young, *Shooting Stars*, pp. 122-125.

[225] Source: Gloria Kamen, *Edward Lear: King of Nonsense*, pp. 37-38.

[226] Source: Paul Terefenko, "David Byrne: Bicycle Diaries." *NOW*. 19-26 October 2009. VOL 29, NO 8. <http://www.nowtoronto.com/books/story.cfm?content=171886>.

[227] Source: Donald J. Sobol, *Encyclopedia Brown's Book of Wacky Cars*, p. 41.

[228] Source: Maria Reidelbach, *Completely MAD*, p. 189.

[229] Source: Michael Foreman, *War Boy: A Country Childhood*, pp. 9, 21, 23, 56, 60, 71.

[230] Source: Louise Cohen, "Terry Frost's life of paint and parties." *The Times*. 22 October 2008 http://entertainment.timesonline.co.uk/tol/arts_and_entertainment/visual_arts/article4986605.ece.

[231] Source: Robin McKown, *The World of Mary Cassatt*, p. 37.

[232] Source: Lauren Collins, "Banksy Was Here: The invisible man of graffiti art." *The New Yorker*. 14 May 2007 <http://www.newyorker.com/reporting/2007/05/14/070514fa_fact_collins>. This is Banksy's Web site: <http://www.banksy.co.uk/>.

[233] Source: Jonathan Jones, "Best of British?" *The Guardian*. 5 July 2007 <http://www.guardian.co.uk/g2/story/0,,2118760,00.html>.

[234] Source: Alexander Theroux, *The Enigma of Al Capp*, p. 48.

[235] Source: Michael Bedard, *William Blake: The Gates of Paradise*, p. 32.

[236] Source: Albert Kostenevich, *Henri Matisse*, pp. 7-8, 60, 63, 89.

[237] Source: Tim Teeman, "The colourful life of Howard Hodgkin." *The Times*. 22 March 2008 <http://entertainment.timesonline.co.uk/tol/arts_and_entertainment/visual_arts/article3567609.ece>.

[238] Source: Stuart A. Kallen, *Claude Monet*, pp. 79-80.

[239] Source: Mark Evanier, *Kirby: King of Comics*, p. 16.

[240] Source: Peggy Thomson, *The Nine-Ton Cat: Behind the Scenes at an Art Museum*, p. 77.

[241] Source: Diana Schultz, editor, *AutobioGraphix*, pp. 19-22.

[242] Source: Martin Sheridan, *Comics and Their Creators: Life Stories of American Cartoonists*, pp. 96-97.

[243] Source: Dean Kamen, "The Smartest Advice I Ever Got: Do What You Love." CNNMoney.com. 22 July 2008 <http://money.cnn.com/galleries/2008/pf/0807/gallery.smartest_advice.moneymag/3.html>.

[244] Source: I.T. Frary, *At Large in Marble Halls*, p. 9.

[245] Source: Martin Sheridan, *Comics and Their Creators: Life Stories of American Cartoonists*, p. 181.

[246] Source: Margot Zemach, *Self-Portrait: Margot Zemach*, pp. 14, 18.

[247] Source: Emine Saner, "Age shall not wither her." *The Guardian*. 18 June 2008 <http://lifeandhealth.guardian.co.uk/women/story/0,,2286088,00.html >.

[248] Source: Jan Greenberg and Sandra Jordan, *Runaway Girl: The Artist Louise Bourgeois*, pp. 48-49.

[249] Source: Robin McKown, *The World of Mary Cassatt*, p. 22.

[250] Source: Dorothy Heiderstadt, *Painters of America*, p. 97.

www.ingramcontent.com/pod-product-compliance
Lightning Source LLC
Chambersburg PA
CBHW051224160726

47994CB00002B/734